MW00678399

Please
Listen
to Me!

A Christian's Guide to

Reflective Listening

Please Listen to Me!

Dick Fetzer

Pleasant Word (a division of WinePress Publishing, PO Box 428, Enumclaw, WA 98022) functions only as book publisher. As such, the ultimate design, content, editorial accuracy, and views expressed or implied in this work are those of the author.

Unless otherwise indicated, all Scripture quotations are taken from the *Holy Bible, New Living Translation,* copyright © 1996. Used by permission of Tyndale House Publishers, Inc., Wheaton, Illinois 60189. All rights reserved.

Scripture references marked KJV are taken from the King James Version of the Bible.

Scripture references marked NASB are taken from the New American Standard Bible, © 1960, 1963, 1968, 1971, 1972, 1973, 1975, 1977 by The Lockman Foundation. Used by permission.

ISBN 13: 978-1-4141-1098-1
ISBN 10: 1-4141-1098-7
Library of Congress Catalog Card Number: 2007907117

Contents

Acknowledgments

My sincere appreciation to:

My loving wife, Joanne Luree Fetzer. I praise God that you are my wife and my best friend. Your consistent encouragement and loving support have enabled me to realize dreams I never thought were possible. Thank you for spending countless hours editing and proofreading. I love you!

My thanks to: Shawn O'Dell who spent many hours proofreading and editing the ever-changing manuscript. Your enthusiasm and insights were an encouragement to me and of great value! Also, my appreciation to Brenda Eberhart, Shelley Kauffman, Jane Keller, Chad Liebert, Stacie Liebert, Steve Rush, Jason Shay, and John Wiley for reviewing the manuscript and offering helpful suggestions and honest critique!

My sincerest appreciation and gratitude to my heavenly Father:

You have blessed me with the desire to learn how to listen. You have ministered to many people as I listened to them and also to You. I thank You for listening to me. You are the Great Listener.

A Word to the Reader

Communicating effectively and teaching others to be more positive in their relationships has been my passion for many years. I share this message with urgency as I weave into the teaching many of my own personal life threads.

The names of the individuals whose true stories I've used have either been changed or used with permission.

To avoid pronoun confusion, indefinite pronouns used in odd-numbered chapters will be masculine. Indefinite pronouns used in even-numbered chapters will be feminine.

Scripture verses used in this book are from the New Living Translation unless otherwise indicated.

In this book I want to illuminate a very important skill in effective communication—that of listening reflectively. This relevant how-to manual provides you with the instruction (and hopefully the incentive) necessary to become someone who listens effectively to the heart of those around you. As you read, perhaps you will recognize yourself as someone who has prevented friends, family members, coworkers or acquaintances from sharing the things that are important to them. Reflective listening is a skill that anyone can learn. It is my prayer that you will be burdened with the desire to become a reflective listener and to show compassion for the needs of others. May you grasp this skill and may it make a wonderful difference in your life and in the lives of the dear souls with whom you live, relate, and even pass briefly by on this journey we call life.

—Dick Fetzer

Chapter One

What *Is* Reflective Listening?

It is false to assume that if one can talk, he can communicate . . .

—Reuel Howe, theologian and educator

The tongue can bring death or life; those who love to talk will reap the consequences.

—Proverbs 18:21

In the fall of 1972, I was invited to attend a series of workshops at a local university. At that time, I was in my sixth year as an elementary teacher and I was also a junior high wrestling coach. Various topics were presented, but one fifteen-minute segment on reflective listening had a tremendous impact upon my life. The instructor encouraged us to learn the skill of reflective listening so we could communicate more effectively with our students.

My initial resistance to his presentation about this structured style of listening was prompted by my belief that I already was a good listener. In fact, I felt certain that I listened better than most people. *Why should I try to follow such a structured procedure?* I thought to myself. *After all, listening is listening. People speak and I listen.*

Throughout the workshop, the instructor patiently taught the skills necessary to reflect back to the speaker what the listener thinks he is hearing. At first, the reflective listening techniques seemed awkward and phony. However, as we practiced the various components of the skill, my resistance decreased and I made two interesting discoveries. First, it became quite evident that I was not the good listener I had thought I was. Second, it felt really good to have someone listen to me when I had an opportunity to speak.

During the final activity of the listening workshop, we worked in small groups to practice our newly learned skill. Each person was asked to relate a personal experience so another member of the group could practice listening reflectively. Fortunately, the woman assigned to listen to me was a guidance counselor who had prior experience with reflective skills. I presented my ongoing concern about not having an assistant wrestling coach. She skillfully listened as I expressed my frustrations with being the only adult in charge of a large group of junior high wrestlers and about having to attend practices or meets while ill because there was no one to assist me. I had approached both the head coach and the principal on several occasions to request an assistant, and each time I had been told that I was doing a fine job of handling the program alone. The compliments and reassurance felt good, however, only for a short time. The fact that my needs and fears were being ignored irritated me. As I described the details of my situation with this skilled listener, it amazed me that she was able to so perceptively pinpoint my feelings.

As the concerns I expressed during this brief listening exercise were reflected back to me, I became aware of just how much this coaching situation had been affecting my health. For the first time, I realized that a stomach ulcer I had suffered from for several months was actually the result of the stress and frustration caused by being solely responsible for the junior high wrestling program. The fact that it took someone skilled in reflective listening just fifteen minutes to help me realize this made a tremendous impact on me. Near the end of the listening experience, I determined that I could not continue to coach unless I had an assistant.

Immediately after the workshop, I went to the principal and informed him that I would resign from my position if he did not hire an assistant coach. Initially, he responded as he had in the past; however, this time I didn't give in. Respectfully, I told him that I had no choice but to resign if he could not find someone to help me within two weeks. Although he tried to persuade me otherwise, I insisted, "I can't do it alone!" Three days later, I had an assistant coach. At that time, I began to realize how powerful the skill of reflective listening could be. I had been held captive by something I didn't know I had the power to change until someone used reflective listening to help set me free. The freedom I gained as a result of this experience inspired me to want to listen to others.

During the next several months, I struggled with listening reflectively. The old habits were hard to break. Occasionally, I remembered to listen; however, there were more times that I forgot. I began to wonder if I would ever become competent as a reflective listener.

Six months after that workshop, I attended a weekend retreat where I was again exposed to reflective listening skills. As a part of the final exercise, I was given the opportunity to be the "listener." The woman I listened to presented a situation in which her friend who was dying of cancer was in denial about her illness. She wanted to know how she could help her friend face the reality of her own death. As she spoke and I reflected, something very interesting took place right before my eyes. At one point, she stopped talking and, after what seemed like a long period of silence, looked up and announced that *she* was the one who was struggling with her friend's illness. Her words surprised everyone in the group: "You know what? I've stayed away from my friend because I didn't know what to say. I'm going to stop by on the way home to honestly tell her how I feel. I want to be there for her."

As the "speaker" in my first experience with reflective listening, I was encouraged to convey my concerns and feelings openly. Someone really listened to me and helped me understand my struggle. I felt validated, and it was so freeing! In my second experience, as the "listener" I saw that I had the power to offer understanding and validation to another person. It was exciting to help someone uncover the truth about herself and gain freedom. This experience increased my determination to work harder to become adept at listening reflectively. I focused on listening to my family, my friends, my students, and even to strangers. Over a period of time, with much practice and perseverance, I did become a better listener.

Since then, I have listened to hundreds of people as they have peeled off the layers of an issue or have dealt with a situation. I continue to be amazed by the fact that reflective listening is so effective in helping someone uncover issues that even he is not aware of. It is such a rewarding journey.

Ironically, though we live in a world of sophisticated communication systems and devices, most of our communication tends to be ineffective. "The more elaborate our means of communication, the less we communicate."[1] We often beat around the bush or talk at each other. A complaint frequently heard is that people "just don't listen." Quite frankly, "the wonder is not that communicating is as difficult as it is, but that it occurs as much as it does."[2]

We are frequently told by communication experts that we need to listen. Spiritual leaders (pastors, priests, rabbis) tell the people in their care to listen to one another. Psychologists and counselors encourage people to listen to one another. These reminders to listen are relevant and much needed, but there is one vital element missing: very few people actually teach others *how* to listen.

Only Hearing Words or Really Listening?

A lot of assumptions are made about listening—especially as it relates to what it is and how it is done. Dr. Tony Alessandra says, "Assuming that just because you can hear, you can listen, is like assuming that just because you can see, you can read." Perhaps the most common misconception we have is that most people are fairly good at listening. In reality, very few people are good listeners because they don't realize that listening is far more than hearing the words that come from the other person.

Three different mental processes are involved in reflective listening. When we listen, we are physically *hearing* the spoken words. At the same time, we are also *thinking* about what the other person is saying. Along with hearing and thinking about what is being said, we are *formulating* our reflective response.

In essence, listening is hearing accurately what the other person is attempting to communicate. Two words are of special importance: the word "accurately" is important because listening effectively enables us to focus on the words and nonverbal actions of the speaker. This gives a clearer understanding of what the speaker is attempting to say. The second word of significance is "attempting." A person is often blind to the feelings, emotions, or real issues of his life. Our ability to reflect back to the speaker what we think he is saying creates a process by which the speaker can focus and convey back to us the real concerns of the situation. Henry David Thoreau said it so well, "It takes two to tell the truth—one to speak and another to hear."

Because reflective listening is a multi-faceted process, there are three basic factors a good listener must fully understand. The first basic factor of reflective listening consists of setting aside our own needs, opinions, experiences, emotions, and advice so that we can truly focus on the person we are listening to. It is very important to set aside self as we listen to another person. This is not easy to do because the issues that others talk with us about often prompt us to think of our own experiences.

The second basic factor of good listening is that we release ourselves from the responsibility of trying to have an answer for the person to whom we are listening. Most of the time, we will not have an answer for that person. The main reason we do not have the answer is that people tend to initially present issues that often are not the real problem.

The third basic factor of reflective listening is that when we listen to someone, it does not mean that we have to agree with that person's ideas or opinions.

If we approach listening with these three thoughts firmly in mind, the listening challenges we face will be easier to overcome.

Being understood and validated is one of the greatest needs we have. Ralph Nichols says it this way: "The most basic of all human needs is the need to understand and be understood. The best way to understand people is to listen to them." When we listen reflectively to someone, we gain an understanding of what he is trying to say through words and body language. As we reflect those feelings and thoughts back to him using the appropriate tone of voice, body posture, and gestures, he will sense that he is understood. Listening reflectively to someone means that we are trying to understand what he is feeling, we accept that he has these feelings and stand by him as he works through an issue.

QUALITIES OF REFLECTIVE LISTENING

There are four specific qualities of reflective listening:

1) Reflective listening is **reflective** because we reflect what we think the speaker is trying to say. It is impossible for us to get into another person's mind and know exactly what he is thinking; however, we can listen carefully and observe his body language as he speaks.

2) Reflective listening is **total** because we listen with our whole being. As a listener, we devote all of our attention to the speaker.

3) Reflective listening is **active** in that we are constantly adjusting to the speaker and concentrating on what he is saying and doing throughout the conversation. We actively follow and respond to the speaker.

4) Reflective listening is **productive** because it usually leads to positive results.

The ability to listen reflectively provides a win-win situation for both the speaker and the listener. The three main purposes and benefits of reflective listening are:

1) It provides the speaker with an opportunity to listen to himself. Many times a person's inner thoughts are deeply hidden or shrouded by strong emotions. It is not until he hears us repeat or reword what he has just said that he actually begins to get in touch with his thoughts and feelings.

2) It provides the speaker with a clearer understanding of his perception of the situation and also of the truth of that situation. By listening to someone and reflecting back to him what he says, we enable him to recognize if there are discrepancies between the two.

3) It provides the listener with a better understanding of what the speaker is trying to

communicate. Who hasn't been misunderstood at one time or another? Not understanding the speaker's intended meaning, or making an assumption, can cause serious problems or hurts in our relationship with that person. Reflecting back to the speaker what we think he has said is an effective tool in minimizing misunderstandings; it gives the speaker an opportunity to clarify his words and their intended meaning.

> If in all our practice of life we could learn to listen . . . . If we could grasp what the other persons are saying as they themselves understand what they are saying, the major hostilities of life would disappear for the simplest reason, that misunderstanding would disappear.
> —Harry Overstreet

Individuals in a casual conversation usually take turns sharing "air time" (talking more or less equally) as they interact. With reflective listening, however, the "air time" is not shared equally. Let's imagine that an ink pen symbolizes "air time." Whoever holds the pen has the right to speak. The objective of reflective listening is to ensure that the speaker holds the pen for a longer period of time and more frequently than the listener. Too often we tend to grab the pen from the other person. However, when we apply reflective listening skills, we are carefully and quickly returning the pen to the speaker, thus keeping the pen in his hand most of the time and preventing ourselves from controlling the conversation.

Not a Casual Conversation

Listening reflectively is different from a casual conversation because we purposefully shift from engaging in casual conversation to listening reflectively at a time when the other person has a strong need to talk, has an issue to resolve, or has an emotion to work through. As we sense the speaker's need to bare his heart or vent his feelings, the focus moves from our own needs and concerns to the needs and concerns of the speaker.

It is also important to listen reflectively before reacting to what the other person says. If we react before attempting to listen reflectively, we will surely open the door to tension and misunderstanding in our relationship with that individual. Conversely, choosing to listen reflectively will provide the opportunity to hear what the other person is attempting to say and will enable us to view the situation from his perspective. It gives us time to set aside our own emotions so that we are better able to focus on the speaker.

The apostle James reminds us to be "quick to listen, slow to speak, and slow to get angry" (James 1:19). When we speak too hastily and without listening to the other person, it is not uncommon for our agitation, frustration, or anger toward that person to quickly escalate. Too late, we realize our mistake and think, *If only I had listened first, it might not have come to this!* The more we try to understand the other person's situation, the less misunderstanding and miscommunication may occur. There is also the decreased chance that anger or other negative emotions will creep in.

Disciplining ourselves to listen first will enable us to enjoy more positive relationships with our spouse, our children, our parents, our coworkers, our friends, and our neighbors. We may even find that listening reflectively can heal fractured relationships. By taking the time to listen to someone, not only are we helping that person work through an issue or express a joy, but we are also providing an opportunity for greater trust and rapport to develop. Charles Dickens said: "No one is useless in this world who lightens the burden of it for anyone else."

Something to think about . . .

Think about a relationship you are currently involved in which would benefit from the use of reflective listening. List the goals you have for improving your communication with that person. Think of several relationships that you would like to work on improving. Ask God to give you the patience and perseverance necessary to become a better listener.

Chapter Two

Our Belief System

I want to hear deeply, clearly, accurately enough
that I am able—to some real extent—to feel what
you feel, hurt a bit where you hurt, and want for
you the freedom to be all you are becoming.
                              —David Augsburger

Let all that you do be done in love.
                    —1 Corinthians 16:14 (NASB)

People sometimes ask, "How long will it take me
to really learn the skill of reflective listening?"
My response to that is, "How badly do you want to
learn it?" Two other important factors that determine
how long it will take for a person to become a reflective listener are 1) **what someone believes about
herself and others** and 2) **the importance we place
on communication.** What we believe about ourselves

and others is called our "belief system." This refers to the values that we have adopted and adhere to. The composite of all the things we believe makes up our belief system. Whether a person chooses to embrace or reject the following six beliefs will either enhance or impede that individual's ability to become a reflective listener.

If we want to become a reflective listener:

(1) We must believe that listening is more about the other person than it is about us.

When someone begins to relate a problem or convey something she is excited about, it is so easy to think of our own experiences and feelings. Though we may think we are responding positively when we talk about our own experiences while listening, this response only serves to shift the focus from the speaker to us.

We all want to be listened to and understood, and it is difficult to refrain from inserting our own experiences into the conversation. However, it is important to keep in mind that we are there for the other person. In listening, it's not about us. Self-centered people rarely become effective listeners because they always manage to shift the focus to themselves rather than allowing the focus to remain on the other person. Each of us has to constantly remind ourselves that we are there to listen. Some people find it helpful to repeat to themselves, "It's not about me . . . . It's not about me . . . . It's not about me . . . ." until it sinks in.

(2) **We must believe that we are not responsible to have the answer or to solve the problem for the person we are listening to.**

Even though embracing this belief should relieve us of responsibility and ultimately lighten our load as listeners, it is actually the second most difficult belief for many would-be listeners to adopt. One reason for this could be that we have been conditioned all of our lives to help those who come to us. The mind quickly thinks of ways that we could offer assistance. As strange as it may seem, the other person usually does not want us to provide an answer for her. And, regardless of what we may think, we often do not have the answer. It is presumptuous to assume that any one of us has the solution or knows the answer to someone else's problem, even though a solution might appear obvious to us. We also need to keep in mind that there is a very good possibility that the issue she has presented thus far is only a presenting problem and not even the real issue. If we cannot relieve ourselves of the responsibility of solving the problem or providing an answer for the speaker, we will have a very difficult time becoming good reflective listeners. Our only responsibility is to be there for the other person. The sooner we realize this, the more quickly we will master the skill of reflective listening.

(3) We must believe that even though reflective listening might seem at first unnatural or fake, it can be one of the greatest skills we will ever learn.

When we begin to apply listening skills, it may feel awkward or unnatural at first. Our mind is consciously thinking about the technique of listening reflectively; therefore, it may seem clinical and impersonal. The truth is that we are probably working harder at listening than ever before. Interestingly, the other person is not aware of what is going on in our mind. Rather, she will sense that she is being heard and validated.

Although reflective listening may be difficult at first, as we practice we will find that the conscious effort eventually becomes an unconscious action. In the same way that learning to ride a bicycle or drive a car requires conscious effort and concentration at first so, too, the application of listening techniques requires much effort initially. Few people give up learning to ride a bike or drive a car because of the effort involved. Those who persevere become quite adept at these skills even though many other distractions demand their attention. The same is true for those who seriously desire to become reflective listeners. If we determine to fight through the "fake" feeling, we will undoubtedly become more effective listeners and communicators.

(4) **We must believe that it is necessary to listen to others without demonstrating an attitude of judgment or condemnation.**

This is a critical belief to embrace because when we judge the speaker or condemn her for her actions, thoughts, or feelings, she will most likely shut down and stop being open with us. In order to listen well, we must suspend judgment and condemnation. In Luke 6:37 we are given this admonition: "Do not judge others, and you will not be judged. Do not condemn others, or it will all come back against you." Mary Field Belenky, consultant on human development, challenges us with this truth: "Really listening and suspending one's own judgment is necessary in order to understand other people on their own terms . . . This is a process that requires trust and builds trust." Listening without judging tends to be especially difficult for individuals who are in positions of authority. If we can focus on listening without entertaining judgmental thoughts toward the speaker regardless of the topic or issue, we will be better equipped to hear her turmoil and feel her pain or joy. It becomes much easier to empathize with someone when we set judgment aside and attempt to understand the emotions she is experiencing.

Empathizing does not mean agreeing with or condoning sinful behavior. Nor does empathizing with the speaker mean that we ignore an issue that needs discipline or correction. But we are to provide a safe place for the individual to explore what is on her heart.

(5) **We must believe that reflective listening can be one of the most spiritual activities we will ever participate in.**

Consequently, this listening skill can also be one of the most evangelistic tools we will ever use. Most people will be more receptive, both to us and to the message of God's love, if first we demonstrate a willingness to validate them by listening to the issues of their hearts.

(6) **Finally, we must believe that a primary purpose for our life is to be committed to loving, caring for, and helping others.**

What we spend our time on is what we believe is important. People are eternal. They alone are what we can take with us from this world into the next. When we reach out to others with compassion and care deeply for them, we are fulfilling the biblical mandate of Matthew 6:20: "Store your treasures in heaven, where moths and rust cannot destroy, and thieves do not break in and steal."

If we are willing to embrace these six beliefs as our own, we are well on the way to becoming reflective listeners.

> How desperately each one of us needs to be heard and understood, especially by the people who are dear to us. And conversely, how vital it is for us to become good listeners in order to meet that need in others.
>
> —James E. Sullivan in *The Good Listener*

In order to change our habits of communication, a two-step process must take place. First, we must have an awareness of the need for change in our communication practices. Second, we must have the desire to change. Old habits die hard, and we must be diligent if we want to replace those habits with newer, healthier ones. It takes a lot of effort and practice. We should not become discouraged if things become harder before they become easier and more rewarding. Unless we are already skilled in reflective listening, we will probably go through a painful time as we gain an awareness of how our former communication practices have negatively affected our relationships with others. We can take heart and be of good cheer because the fact that we are aware is the first step in making the necessary changes that we need to make.

How long will it take to really learn the skill of reflective listening? It depends on how badly we want to learn it and how hard we are willing to work to achieve it.

Something to think about . . .

Think about your belief system. How does the information presented in this chapter compare to what you have believed about listening? In what ways is your belief system the same? In what ways is it different from what you've read here?

Chapter Three

Stumbling Blocks to Effective Communication

When people talk, listen completely. Most people never listen.

—Ernest Hemingway

Everyone enjoys a fitting reply; it is wonderful to say the right thing at the right time!

—Proverbs 15:23

One of the most important roles of an effective communicator is to offer an environment in which the speaker can speak openly and honestly from the heart. Anything that prevents the speaker's thoughts from flowing freely during the conversation is called a "stumbling block." There are ten stumbling blocks to effective communication. It is necessary for us to think about them before we look at the "how" of reflective listening. Being aware of the stumbling blocks to effective communication is vital to our success in learning the skill of reflective listening. Each of the stumbling blocks has a different negative effect upon the listening process.

Often these stumbling blocks are learned at a very young age from those around us. Most people believe that giving advice, asking questions, or talking about a friend who is in a similar situation is a great way to listen. In reality, the opposite is true. These actions almost always create barriers to effective communication and impede positive relationships.

The following behaviors are the most common stumbling blocks:

1. Asking questions[1]
2. Giving advice[2]
3. Answering questions
4. Telling the speaker "I know exactly how you feel"
5. Self-editorializing
6. Changing the subject
7. Attempting to reassure the speaker[3]
8. Pretending to listen
9. Not attending the speaker
10. Not providing the proper physical setting

Let's take a close look at each one —

1. ASKING QUESTIONS

Undoubtedly, the number one stumbling block that well-intentioned listeners struggle with is that of asking questions. Many who have seriously attempted to improve their listening skills have admitted that this is a primary temptation. The question-asking stumbling block is the most common and one of the greatest inhibitors of effective listening.

There are two basic reasons why we ask questions. First, we are trained at a young age to use question asking as a tool to gain information or to express our interest. As a result, asking questions comes naturally to most of us. By the time we reach adulthood, we are experts at asking questions. We have been taught to believe that the more questions we ask, the more interest we are showing. Though a popular assumption, this is not necessarily true. Ironically, question asking often serves only to hinder the person who is attempting to express his story or feelings.

Second, we feel responsible to provide a solution or give an answer in order to help the speaker. So instead of truly listening, we focus on gaining as much information as possible in order to give the speaker our best advice. As a result, the conversation very quickly becomes focused on us and what we hope to gain rather than on the speaker and his needs at that moment.

Why is question asking so detrimental to the listening process? One reason is that question asking tells the speaker that the answers to our questions are more important to us than what the speaker wants to say. Many of our questions are actually irrelevant to the real issue. A second reason why question asking can be detrimental to the listening process is that it puts the listener in control of the conversation. Unfortunately, for many would-be listeners, this is more comfortable than being at the mercy of the speaker. In order for effective communication to take place, however, we must allow the speaker to be in control of the conversation. As listeners, we must allow the speaker to decide what information and, specifically, how much he wants to reveal. The speaker needs to be at the helm of the conversation. We go where the speaker leads without attempting to direct him.

Being presented with a question forces the speaker's thoughts to come to a complete stop and change direction in order to formulate an answer. Questions interrupt the natural flow of thought and speech. Both the speaker and the listener are now off track. As a matter of fact, the speaker might never return to the same point in the conversation. Questions also seem to have a way of stimulating more questions. It doesn't take long for a would-be listener to become more concerned (even consumed!) with asking the questions that enter his mind than with listening to the speaker. Questions also serve to move the speaker and the listener farther and farther away from the initial issue. The temptation to ask questions can be so overwhelming that it actually prevents us from hearing the speaker at all! Every person who truly desires to be an effective listener must eliminate question asking.

During our communication skills training seminars, my wife and I request that participants refrain from asking any questions when they are practicing reflective listening skills. The first concern would-be listeners have about this no question stance is, "How will I find out what I need to know in order to help the person?" We emphasize that when the listener refrains from asking questions, the speaker is allowed to move into levels of sharing that he would probably not reach if he had to stop to answer questions. We need to remember that it's not about having the answer or solving the problem. The greatest help we can give the speaker is to get out of the way and allow him to express himself without interruption. Frequently, individuals will stop abruptly in the middle of a conversation and say, "I don't know why I'm telling you all of this." Very likely, it is because the listener has permitted them to talk without interruption and did not take control of the conversation by pumping them with questions.

It is difficult to enter into a conversation and strive to not ask any questions. Unless we are skilled reflective listeners, it is very likely that we will quickly identify with those who have discovered how difficult it really is to not ask questions at all. For those who struggle with asking questions, be assured that continued proper practice of reflective listening will be so rewarding that receiving answers to a few questions really will be insignificant.

Questions will inevitably come to our minds as we are listening. This is a very normal and natural function of the brain. However, our task is to resist the temptation to voice those questions. Instead, we put them aside and focus solely on what the speaker is attempting to communicate. This will take some practice and perseverance, but we'll be glad we did it!

2. GIVING ADVICE

The second stumbling block to effective listening is that of giving advice. This is a common problem, especially for someone in a position of authority over the person who is attempting to share, such as parents, teachers, managers, supervisors, and spiritual leaders. Giving advice is also common among concerned friends and others who feel they must fix the situation.

Many people challenge the validity of giving advice as a stumbling block because the assumption is that the speaker has come to them for advice. And, very often, this will appear to be the case. However, the person who presents a problem frequently has the answer to his own problem—although he may not be aware of it. Often, when the speaker begins to talk, the listener will listen for a short period of time until he thinks he has an understanding of the problem. He then stops listening and begins to formulate an answer. It is extremely difficult to listen effectively and formulate an answer simultaneously. The listener waits only long enough for the speaker to stop talking (or to just take a breath) so that he can quickly solve the speaker's problem with his well-thought-out solution or advice.

> There are people who, instead of listening to what is being said to them, are already listening to what they are going to say themselves.
>
> —Albert Guinon

Giving advice could be effective if the listener had a total grasp and understanding of the speaker's real issue or concern. However, the majority of the people tend to present an issue that is not the real issue. Dr. Robert Bolton in his book *People Skills* calls this initial presentation the presenting problem (p. 69). In some instances, the speaker might be, consciously or unconsciously, testing the listener with a safe issue—presenting a problem that is not as deep as the real issue. In other cases, the speaker may not be aware that the presenting problem is not the main issue. Unfortunately, when the listener gives advice about a presenting problem, both the listener and the speaker may initially feel some satisfaction. The listener feels good because he gave what seemed like good, sound advice. The speaker may initially be satisfied because the listener did address the presenting problem. However, because the real issue was not presented, the speaker will not likely heed the advice given, or will continue to come back to the listener, or will go to others for support, or will feel alone because no one really understood his situation. Two examples of real-life situations will illustrate what can happen when a listener is focused on solving the speaker's problem and giving advice as opposed to what can happen when the listener refrains from offering advice.

Near the end of a seminar on reflective listening, I asked for a volunteer to share a concern so I could demonstrate the listening skills. As I listened, Pam moved into more serious issues. During a period of silence, I noticed that she was nervously rubbing her hands together. Immediately, I gave her permission to stop speaking. As soon as I did, Nikki, a participant in the training group, started giving Pam advice on how to handle her problem. Nikki had decided on a solution to Pam's presenting problem and, at that point, had stopped listening. Consequently, she never realized that Pam had moved on to a more serious issue. Nikki rambled on about the solution that she had chosen for Pam. To spare Nikki from embarrassment, I quickly summarized some of the important issues I had heard Pam mention and ended the session.

In the second situation, Marilyn told Jane that she was overwhelmed by the many projects she wanted to work on during the summer break from teaching. She spoke about her frustration at not being able to take a vacation because she didn't have time. As Jane listened, she was tempted to tell Marilyn which projects were really not that important. Instead she used reflective listening skills. As Marilyn continued to talk, Jane noticed how excited Marilyn was becoming. By the end of their conversation, Marilyn had found her own solution to the dilemma. She had decided to postpone her vacation until the following year and had prioritized her projects so she could still have time for the activities she enjoyed. By not giving advice, Jane simply allowed Marilyn to peel off the layers of the proverbial onion and arrive at her own solution.

It is absolutely crucial that we ignore the urge to give advice as we listen to others.

3. ANSWERING QUESTIONS

Stumbling block number three is answering questions. Answering questions actually can hinder effective communication. Here lies one of the unique phenomena of communication: Often an individual will ask us a question as a test to see if we will listen. Unconsciously, he is hoping that by asking a question, a door will be opened for him to talk about his need. Unfortunately, too many would-be listeners answer the question, thus taking immediate control of the communication experience and closing that door. As a result, the person who asks the question very quickly becomes the listener instead of the speaker.

One Saturday in October my son, Rick, who was a high school junior and a member of the football team, asked what I would do if he got into a fight at school. I quickly proceeded to give him my opinion about fighting and described the consequences he would face. After my lecture, I said, "I'm curious about why you asked." He replied, "I was just wondering."

One month later, I discovered that Rick had gotten into a fight on a Monday morning following the last football game of the season. I sat down with him and encouraged him to explain what had happened. He told me about a boy who had badgered him all season by tripping him in the hall, throwing food at him in the cafeteria, and calling him names. That boy knew that if Rick got into a fight, he would be kicked off the football team. Rick told me that he had gone to his coaches and an administrator for help. They all told him to stay out of any fights or he would be kicked off the team. After he explained his story to me, I asked why he did not come to me for help. His answer was, "I did!" That October morning he had talked with his father. Sadly, I had answered his question without first listening to him. This personal experience has frequently reminded me that we need to be very careful about answering questions.

4. **TELLING THE SPEAKER "I KNOW EXACTLY HOW YOU FEEL"**

A statement such as "I know exactly how you feel" will quickly shut down the speaker. Seemingly innocuous, and intended to be helpful, this statement quickly closes the door to effective communication. Some people will argue that saying "I know just how you feel" convinces the speaker that we are listening to him, and even identifying with him. The reality is that this statement, and those similar to it, has the opposite effect.

There are two profound reasons why a listener should never say, "I know exactly how you feel," or any other similar statement that is known to close the door to effective listening. First, it is not true. Since we are all unique and various factors are involved in our different experiences, no one can ever really know exactly how another person feels in any given situation. Erin Linn in her book *I Know Just How You Feel . . . avoiding the clichés of grief* warns: "No one knows how another person feels, because we are not that person, and we cannot know the depth of their feelings in any given circumstance any more than they can know ours . . . . Sometimes we think we do, but we may not even be close."[4] For example, two people might each experience a major loss in their lives such as the death of a loved one. Each one brings to that situation different experiences, emotions, backgrounds, support, and faith, and, as a result, each person's reaction to the same situation is very different. For one to tell the other, "I know exactly how you feel" is more hurtful than helpful. Sometimes a speaker will adamantly say, "You do not know how I feel!" He is correct. We do not know how he feels. And, if we have ever been the recipient of such a comment, perhaps we can recall the anger and frustration we may have felt.

> The heart of another is a dark forest, always, no matter how close it has been to one's own.
> —Willa Cather

The second reason why this statement closes the door to effective communication is that it tells the speaker that there is no longer any reason for him to continue speaking. The assumption that we already know how the speaker feels makes it unnecessary for the speaker to continue.[5] Rather than shutting down the speaker, there are some phrases we can use that will encourage the person to continue speaking. We could say to someone, "I really do not have any idea how that made you feel." This keeps the door wide open for him to tell us how it made him feel. We could also say, "I cannot pretend to know how you feel about that." The individual will respect and appreciate our honesty. Unfortunately, the "I know how you feel" statement is often followed by the next stumbling block.

5. SELF-EDITORIALIZING

Self-editorializing occurs when the listener becomes the speaker in order to insert his own experience, thus forcing the speaker to become the listener. People who are guilty of this behavior defend themselves by arguing that sharing their personal experience will convince the speaker that they (the listener) really do understand. In this case, the listener appears to have a need to identify with the speaker. Unfortunately, the speaker often becomes frustrated or angry because something very personal and perhaps sensitive to him is abruptly taken out of his hands. Instead of talking, he is required to listen to someone else's experience and is never given the opportunity to express his feelings.

It's not about us. Anything we do that shifts the focus from the speaker to ourselves must be avoided. Telling our own story to someone who has recently gone through a seemingly similar experience can actually be detrimental to our relationship with that individual. Do not give in to the temptation to relate personal experiences!

6. CHANGING THE SUBJECT

There are times, after the speaker has begun to talk, when the listener might be tempted to change the subject. This is a subtle way of controlling the conversation and should be avoided because it does not allow the speaker to talk naturally.

One reason the listener might change the subject is that it makes him feel uncomfortable to talk about (or listen to) a particular topic. For example, if the speaker talks about the loss of a loved one, and the situation evokes sad or uncomfortable memories of a loss that the listener has experienced, it is often tempting to try to divert the speaker's attention to something that is more comfortable for the listener. In other situations, the listener might be tempted to move on to something that will make the speaker feel more comfortable. However, keep in mind that it does not help the speaker work through the problem if the conversation is diverted to another topic.

7. REASSURING THE SPEAKER

The primary reason a listener may be tempted to reassure the speaker is to make him feel better. Some examples of reassuring phrases are:

- "Don't worry. Everything will work out."
- "You're resourceful. You can handle it!"
- "It's not your fault."
- "You did a great job."
- "Next week at this time you won't even remember this."

Serious would-be listeners sometimes struggle with the thought that reassuring someone who is experiencing a negative emotion can be a stumbling block. They often ask, "How can reassuring a person possibly be a stumbling block? After all, I'm only trying to help." Ironically, when we reassure someone we fail to validate that person's feelings. We are essentially telling him to "keep your chin up" when what he really needs is a shoulder to cry on. People generally do not want to receive a pat on the back and be told "You can do it" or "You're doing a wonderful job" when they are feeling overwhelmed. They need to be heard. They need to know that someone hears and validates their feelings, however sad or awful those feelings might be.

In Ephesians 4:29 we find a powerful reminder about encouragement: "Let everything you say be good and helpful, so that your words will be an encouragement to those who hear them." Untimely reassurances are not, in most cases, encouraging. The most helpful thing we can do for another person is to validate his feelings by listening to him.

MATT'S STORY

Matt worked for a local newspaper as the distribution manager. As the company grew, Matt's responsibilities increased. The stress level was affecting his health. He went to his supervisor to ask for help, but his supervisor assured him that he was doing a great job. In fact, he gave Matt a pay raise! Several months later, Matt again approached his supervisor and told him that the workload was too much for him to handle without additional help. This time his supervisor gave him a company car. It would appear that the supervisor was being helpful. In reality, Matt felt that his supervisor was disregarding his concerns and ignoring his cry for help. After months of struggling with his extensive workload, Matt went to his supervisor a third time—this time to submit his resignation letter. He accepted a job elsewhere with less money, less stress, and no company car. Reassurance and perks were not what he was seeking, nor did they solve his problem.

When I was a coach, being told that I was doing a great job only served to further frustrate me. Much of my frustration resulted from the realization that the issues I presented were not being heard. It felt to me as if my concerns and feelings were not important to the other person and nothing constructive was done to help me, at least not at first.

Quickly reassuring another person during a listening experience is ineffective and closes the door to communication. We must keep in mind at all times that the concern presented initially is most likely not the real or underlying problem. A reassuring response often prevents the speaker from going deeper into the issue. It might even compound his original situation by causing him to feel guilty or condemned for feeling or thinking the way he does! Reassuring basically serves to make the listener feel better; however, it does not help the speaker. Here is an admonition from the book of Proverbs: "Singing cheerful songs to a person with a heavy heart is like taking someone's coat in cold weather or pouring vinegar in a wound" (Proverbs 25:20).

Is there any time when we may reassure the speaker? There may definitely be some times in which reassuring the other person is appropriate; however, the listener should feel comfortable about reassuring the speaker when—and only when—the listener is sure that the speaker has arrived at the real issue. We have to be extremely careful in offering reassurance because we might not yet have reached the real problem. Be cautious when reassuring someone. Ask yourself, "Am I reassuring the other person to help *him* or am I reassuring him to make *myself* feel better?"

8. PRETENDING TO LISTEN

There are times when we will be approached by someone who wants or needs our attention. If we are busy, it is tempting to continue our work and nod our head or say something to give the impression that we are listening.

Pretending to listen is one of the worst things a person can do because it fosters superficial communication. People who pretend to listen create an atmosphere of distrust. They seem phony. If we only pretend to listen, we are sending the message that what the other person is saying is not as important as what we are doing, at least not at that moment. It has the potential to make the other person feel that we don't really care about him or what he is saying.

When a child comes home from school and the parent is preparing dinner, the child wants to relate some exciting news. The parent attempts to listen while preparing the meal but it doesn't take the child long to feel as if preparing dinner is more important to the parent than what happened at school that day. When someone senses that he is not being listened to, he can easily feel that he is not loved.

Both we and the speaker will benefit if we honestly let him know that we cannot listen to him at that time or in that place. It would be best to ask if we could meet at a more convenient time so we could give him our undivided attention. However, if we can tell by the other person's demeanor that his concern or issue is urgent, it might be necessary to stop what we are doing and give him our full attention.

Whatever we do, we don't pretend to listen. That will only minimize the seriousness of the speaker's situation. At the very least, our pretending to listen will negatively affect our relationship with him.

9. NOT ATTENDING THE SPEAKER

The most effective component of communication is what we say with our bodies as we listen. Not attending the speaker is similar to pretending to listen. The difference is that the listener may be saying the appropriate words but is not responding with the proper body language. Many times this occurs because we are preoccupied when approached by someone who needs us to listen. Often, people do not give the speaker proper attention because they have not been taught the importance of body language. Concentrating on eye contact, posture and tone of voice are only a few of the ways we can listen more effectively.

Reflective listening requires that we fully attend the speaker!

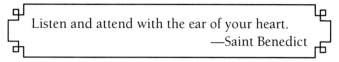

Listen and attend with the ear of your heart.
—Saint Benedict

10. NOT PROVIDING THE PROPER PHYSICAL SETTING

Not providing the proper physical setting goes hand-in-hand with not attending the speaker and is just as important. We must be aware that both the listener and the speaker need to have the proper physical setting if reflective listening is to occur. This includes privacy and freedom from distractions. We have more control of the physical setting than we might realize. Listening in a noisy crowded room, in the presence of a blaring radio or television, or in a group where others might undermine reflective listening, should be avoided. A distraction-free location in which both the listener and the speaker are comfortable and where we can give the speaker our undivided attention is ideal.

Alison and Beth had planned to meet at a local restaurant for lunch. The restaurant was crowded and the tables were close together. Alison could tell from Beth's body language that something was really bothering her. Yet Beth seemed to be more comfortable discussing superficial issues. After an hour, the crowd thinned out and there were fewer distractions. As the tables near them emptied, Beth's willingness to discuss deeper issues became evident and Alison was able to listen as Beth divulged some serious marital problems. She realized that Beth needed more privacy and a quieter environment before she felt safe talking about something so personal. Fortunately, Alison was patient and waited for Beth to feel comfortable enough to open up more fully.

A WORD OF ENCOURAGEMENT

Individuals often express a sense of guilt or are overwhelmed and sometimes even shocked to learn how they may have damaged relationships with others by using one of these stumbling blocks. It can be quite devastating to discover how we may have unknowingly hurt rather than helped another person. But we will become better equipped to help others as we learn how to listen reflectively, and our use of the stumbling blocks will decrease.

Something to think about . . .

Which stumbling blocks do you find yourself using most of the time?
What will you do to avoid these stumbling blocks in your communication with others?

Chapter Four

Changing
Questions Into
Statements

We never listen when we are eager to speak.
—Luise von Francois

We can be mirrors that brightly reflect the glory
of the Lord . . . .
—2 Corinthians 3:18 (The Living Bible)

The temptation to ask questions is the most difficult hurdle for listeners to overcome. Therefore, it is imperative to revisit the stumbling block of asking questions. If we are going to become reflective listeners, we must learn to change those questions that naturally come to our mind into statements.

As we stated in Chapter 3, questions will inevitably come to our minds as we are listening. This is a normal function of the brain. However, in

41

order to ensure effective communication, we need to resist the temptation to voice those questions. Since the listening experience focuses on the speaker, we must demonstrate a greater interest in the speaker's concerns than in our desire to have our questions answered. Rather than using questions to steer the conversation, we need to relinquish control and allow the speaker to lead the way. The skill of changing questions into statements for the purpose of listening reflectively requires practice and perseverance, but will result in effective communication.

Although we might argue that asking questions is one way to demonstrate our interest in what the speaker is conveying, a skilled listener can actually communicate more effectively by using statements rather than questions. This is because the brain responds differently to a question than it does to a statement. Questions interrupt the natural flow of thought and speech. When the speaker is presented with a question, she is forced to abruptly stop mid-thought or mid-speech and her brain must "shift gears" in order to formulate an answer. As a result, both the speaker and the listener are now off track, and the speaker might never return to the same point in the conversation. The practice of asking the speaker questions may impede or even bring the conversation to a complete stop. Therefore, it becomes crucial that we learn to change questions into statements.

During our communication skills training seminars, my wife Joanne and I stand at opposite sides of the room to visually demonstrate for participants what occurs in the thought process when we ask questions. The objective is for me (the speaker) to walk toward Joanne (the listener) as we interact. I begin to walk toward her as I speak. (Effective communication draws people together, thus closing the emotional distance between listener and speaker.) As she reflects, I continue to walk slowly toward her. However, any time she asks me a question, I immediately stop walking. If she asks two questions in a row, I take a step backward. Each time the listener asks a question, the speaker must stop and consciously think of a response. Once the speaker has responded to the question, and any other subsequent questions that are presented, it becomes harder for the listener to encourage the speaker to regroup her thoughts and continue the conversation.

Indeed, the practice of changing questions into statements may require a major adjustment in our thinking and may not be easy at first; however, it will have a positive impact upon our communication. We will be amazed at the ease with which the listener talks when we refrain from interrupting her with our agenda of inquiries. Let's take a look at how this is possible.

In order to encourage the other person to speak openly with us, we need to be willing to use a gentle, invitational approach. Most questions can be restated in a less invasive way and presented to the speaker in a statement format. Changing a question into a statement greatly increases the potential for positive interaction to take place between the speaker and the listener. Let's consider how differently the speaker might respond to a statement such as "It looks to me as if you're upset" or "I sense that something is bothering you" as opposed to the less tactful use of questions such as "What are you so upset about?" or "What's bothering you?" The following examples of questions and the statements they have been changed into further helps to illustrate this point.

Question A: "Why did you buy that car?"
Statement A: "You must have had a good reason for buying that car."
Question B: "How did you ever get into that situation?"
Statement B: "I'd be interested in how that happened."
Question C: "When did he call you?"
Statement C: "I'm not sure I heard you say what time he called."
Question D: "What was she doing there?"
Statement D: "I'm curious as to why she was there."

In each of the examples presented above, the speaker is likely to respond with the same information. However, the flow of her thoughts is not interrupted when she is presented with a statement rather than a question. We need to keep in mind that a question generally *demands* a response, whereas a statement *invites* a response.

Let's take a look at four examples of typical conversations where the would-be listener initially responds to the body language of the speaker by asking questions. The negative result of this approach is not uncommon in many relationships. It will be interesting to see how the mood of each interaction changes as the would-be listener changes the question to a statement of observation.

Julie, a ninth grader, gets off the bus and walks slowly with her head down. It is evident that something is bothering her. Her mother, Brenda, can easily read her daughter's body language as Julie reaches the porch. Brenda immediately begins to question her. "What's wrong? What happened at school?"

Julie retorts, "Nothing's wrong. Why are you so nosy all the time? Leave me alone!"

Brenda throws her hands up and shouts in frustration, "What did I do wrong? I just wanted to know what happened at school today."

Neither mother nor daughter speaks the rest of the evening as a result of what took place when Julie got off the bus. This is not an uncommon parent-child interaction. Look at the same situation again, this time without the questions from Mom.

Julie gets off the bus and walks slowly toward the porch with her head down. Brenda quickly notices her body language. The questions begin to rush to her mind; however, she immediately changes those questions to a statement of observation.

"Hi, Sweetheart." She pauses before continuing. "It looks like something's bothering you."

Brenda reacts this time with a statement that reflects Julie's body language. There is a much greater chance that Julie will not become offended and explode when approached with a statement rather than multiple questions.

Here's another scenario in which Kyle, a twelfth grader, is being picked up at school by his father, Mike. Kyle looks thoughtful as he climbs into the passenger seat. Mike notices Kyle's expression.

Mike: "What's bothering you, son?"

Kyle: "Nothing."

Mike: "Come on, I can tell you're thinking about something—it's written all over your face. What's bugging you?"

Kyle: "Dad, nothing's bugging me. Why are you always prying into my business?"

The silence is deafening for the rest of the ride home.

Let's give Mike a second chance. Kyle gets into the car with a thoughtful look on his face. This time Mike changes his question to a statement of observation.

Mike: "It looks like you're thinking about something."

Again, there is a much better chance that Kyle will be open to sharing his thoughts if approached in a noninvasive, non-threatening manner.

The third scenario focuses on Faith and Jerry, a young couple who have been married for five years.

The communication between them is tentative. Faith asks a lot of questions. She says that it's the only way she can get Jerry to talk. One night Jerry comes home from work looking angry. Faith is preparing dinner as Jerry enters the kitchen. Faith sees Jerry's expression and reacts:

Faith: "Hon, what's bothering you?"

Jerry: "Nothing. I'm just tired."

Faith: "I can tell something is bugging you. What is it?"

Jerry: "Nothing—I told you!"

Jerry walks out to the garage and tinkers with the lawn mower. Later, they eat supper in silence. The rest of the evening is quiet with Faith fretting while Jerry sits silently and gazes at the television.

Let's rewind and give Faith the opportunity to invite Jerry to open up.

Jerry walks into the kitchen looking angry.

Faith: "It looks like you're upset, Hon."

The prospects of an effective conversation have just greatly increased.

In this next scenario, good friends Steph and Diane run into each other at the local grocery store. Steph can see by Diane's expression that she is troubled.

Steph: "Diane, what's wrong?"

Diane: (with tears in her eyes) "Nothing."

Steph: "I can see that something is bothering you! We're friends—You can tell me. What is it?"

Diane hesitates briefly before responding, "I'm fine . . . really." She then quickly changes the subject by asking Steph, "How's your new job?"

Now Steph is going to rewind and do that again:

Steph: "Diane, it looks as if something's bothering you."

It will be interesting to see where this conversation goes as a result of Steph's ability to invite rather than invade.

The listener in each scenario chose to state what the other person's body language seemed to be indicating to him or her. Likewise, it's very important that each listener practices ways to change the questions that come naturally to mind into statements that express what we observe about the other person's body language. Once we master this skill, we are ready to learn the reflective listening process.

We can enter into a reflective listening situation in many ways. Often it will take place when a child comes home from school (Julie and Brenda), a parent picks up a teen at school (Mike and Kyle), a spouse comes home from work (Jerry and Faith), or when two people casually meet (Steph and Diane). The listeners in our scenarios observed the speaker's body language and identified a specific emotion. The questions that came to mind were changed to statements. These statements were the first step in an important process in the reflective listening process: the invitation to talk.

Something to think about . . .

Here's how you can take action. Practice changing the following questions to statements.

- How old is she?
- Where did he say he is going after graduation?
- Why did she yell at you?
- Who else was at the meeting?
- Why did you get angry at her?
- What did he do when you said that?
- Were you happy?
- How did that make you feel?
- Who told you that?
- When are you going to fix the garage door?

Chapter Five

The Invitation to Talk: Do's and Don'ts

If you listened hard enough the first time, you might have heard what I meant to say.
—Unknown

Though good advice lies deep within the heart, a person with understanding will draw it out.
—Proverbs 20:5

It is important to realize that the atmosphere that is created during the first several seconds of interaction between two people can set the stage for the next several hours. One of the most effective ways to initiate a positive conversation is by using the "invitation to talk." This approach is especially helpful when the other person appears to be experiencing strong emotion.

The "invitation to talk" is what Dr. Robert Bolton refers to in his book *People Skills* as a "door opener."[1] A well-executed invitation to talk literally opens the door to increased and effective communication.

When two people first meet, the invitation to talk consists of three important steps. The first step is to "observe the body language" of the speaker and verbally reflect what he appears to be saying non-verbally. We must remember that we are not necessarily stating a fact, but simply our perception of the situation. In order to relate to the speaker that we are reflecting what we *think* he is demonstrating, it is best to begin our statement of observation with phrases such as:

- "It appears that . . ."
- "I sense . . ."
- "You seem . . ."
- "It looks to me like . . ."

By applying the skill of changing questions to statements, the question "What did you do this time?" can be softened by saying "It looks like something is bothering you." The question "Why are you sad?' could be restated as "You seem troubled." Each statement is a sensitive response to the other person's body language or tone of voice. The act of changing invasive questions into observations of the other person's nonverbal actions is vital to creating an atmosphere in which the speaker feels comfortable to talk.

The second step of the invitation to talk is the "prompt." The would-be listener prompts the would-be speaker to tell him more. It is important to phrase the prompt as a statement rather than a question. The prompt is a statement that lets the speaker know that we are interested and willing to listen. Examples of prompting are: "I'd like to hear about it" or "I'm here if you want to talk." These are soft and inviting statements.

During our training seminars, my wife and I give participants the opportunity to practice the three steps of the "invitation to talk" as I leave the room and enter again displaying body language that indicates a particular emotion. Each person creates a statement that reflects what he or she thinks I am conveying by my body language. After writing this reflective statement, the participants are then asked to write a prompt to invite the speaker to talk. This is where many people struggle. Rather than phrasing the prompt as a statement, questions bombard their minds. They want to ask, "What happened?"; "Can you tell me about it?"; "Do you want to talk about it?"; "Is there something you would like to share?" By the time I enter the room the third time, many participants are able to form their invitations into gentle, noninvasive statements such as "I'm here if you'd like to talk"; "I'd be interested in hearing more about that" or "If you want to talk, I'm willing to listen." It is hard for the speaker to resist talking when we gently invite "I sense that something is bothering you" (response to the body language) and "I'm here if you want to share" (prompt).

The third step of the invitation to talk is a "period of silence." This occurs when the would-be listener gives the speaker time to consider the invitation. This period of time is vital in showing respect for the speaker by giving him space. Fifteen to twenty seconds of silence is an adequate amount of time to allow the other person to think and to respond. He will either accept or decline the invitation. Whatever his choice, it is *very* important that we respect his decision. Too often someone will give an invitation and then pressure the other person to speak even after he has declined. Statements such as, "Come on! You can tell me" or "You really should get it off your chest" do not demonstrate respect toward the individual and will often serve only to push him farther away. After the listener-trainees in our seminars state what they observe, offer the prompt and wait in silence, it is very easy for me to want to talk. This is what effective communication is all about. We are well on our way to becoming reflective listeners when the other person finds it easy to tell us what is on his mind.

Many times when my children were young, I would respond to their nonverbal cues when they came home from school. One instance involved my then 15-year-old daughter. After getting off the bus, she walked in the front door with a troubled look on her face. My initial reaction to her body language was "It looks like something is bothering you." She glanced at me as she walked toward the refrigerator to get a snack. I offered the prompt: "I'm here if you want to talk about it." After a period of silence, she responded, "No, I'm just tired." Even though I sensed that something was bothering her, I respected her decision. Later that evening, she came to me and spoke freely about an argument she had had with her boyfriend that day. This provided an opportunity for me to listen and reflect as she talked.

Productive parent-child discussions are more frequent when we treat our children with respect and do not attempt to pry into their personal lives. We allow the other person to talk with us when he is ready.

A Second Visit

Let's revisit each of the earlier scenarios.

Julie walks onto the porch slowly with her head down. Brenda remembers to focus on what she is observing.

Brenda: "Hi, Sweetheart. It looks like something's bothering you. I'm here if you want to talk about it." Brenda allows time for Julie to respond. She is going to respect whatever Julie says.

Julie: "Mary told me I was stupid because I failed the math quiz this morning."

Now, let's see how Mike and Kyle are doing:

Kyle climbs into the passenger seat looking thoughtful.

Mike: "It looks as if you've got a lot on your mind. I'd be interested in hearing about it." Mike waits respectfully as his son decides how to respond to his invitation.

Kyle: "Larry says he is going to join the Air Force after graduation. Dad, do you think I should go to college or join the Air Force?"

As we look in on Faith and Jerry, she is cooking dinner as Jerry enters the kitchen. Faith sees Jerry's face and says, "It looks like you're upset, Hon. I'm willing to listen." She gives Jerry time to decide how to respond to her invitation.

Jerry: "My boss told me today that I'm not doing a good job. He should talk. I have to clean up his messes all the time!"

Steph and Diane meet at the local grocery store. Diane looks worried.

Steph: "Diane, it looks like something's bothering you. I'm here if you need to talk." She allows time for Diane to respond.

Diane: "I'm okay . . . I just have a lot on my mind, I guess."

Steph: "You're telling me that you've got a lot to deal with right now."

Diane: "Yes, I do! I'm just not sure what to do about Jessica. Her teacher says she keeps picking on a girl in her class."

Steph is determined to stay with her friend and help her work through this issue. We will join them again later.

The Invitation to Talk: Do's and Don'ts

We have discussed the three basic steps to an invitation to talk, which include stating what we observe about the other person's body language, prompting him to be open with us, and providing silence. When Brenda, Mike, Faith, and Steph respond to the nonverbal clues, provide a prompt, and wait patiently, it greatly increases the probability of effective communication.

RESUMING A PREVIOUS CONVERSATION

A situation in which two people meet to resume an earlier conversation should be handled differently. The listener should begin the conversation by restating a fact or a feeling that was mentioned during the previous interaction. An example of an invitation to talk in this case might be: "The last time we talked, you mentioned your mother's illness. I'm curious how she is feeling." As always, we allow time for the person to decide whether to accept or decline our invitation. A second example of using an invitation to talk is: "The other day you said that you were frustrated with your son's teacher. I'm interested in how things are going." We must be sure to phrase the invitation as a statement, not a question. After giving an invitation to talk and a prompt, we allow time for the other person to respond and then respect his decision.

The following scenario illustrates how an invitation to talk can be used to resume a previous conversation.

Zach and Kevin had engaged in casual conversation at the men's monthly prayer breakfast. As their conversation progressed, Zach spoke about the frustration he was having with his secretary over work-related issues. Kevin noted that Zach seemed tense as he talked about this situation, and he began to listen reflectively. Unfortunately, their conversation was interrupted. Kevin decided it was important to follow up with Zach, so he arranged to meet him for breakfast at Kelly's Café the following week. Here's how Kevin handles the initial part of that second meeting.

Kevin: "Zach, the last time we talked, you mentioned that you felt your secretary was not doing her job. I'm interested in hearing more about that."

Kevin did not begin with a question. Instead, he focused on an important issue that Zach had presented during their previous conversation. Kevin's statement opens the door for Zach to talk if he feels comfortable and chooses to do so. He gives Zach time to consider the invitation.

Zach: (sighs) "I'm just not sure what to do . . ."

In any conversation, the use of reflective listening allows the speaker to talk openly.

The Invitation to Talk: Do's and Don'ts

Something to think about . . .

Here's how you can take action.
Practice changing these questions into statements of observation. Remember to preface each statement with words such as "I sense . . ."; "It seems . . ."; "You look . . ."; "It appears . . ."

- "What's bothering you?"
- "Why are you crying?"
- "What are you smiling about?"
- "Why such a glum look?'
- "What happened to make you so excited?"
- "Who upset you?"

Practice changing the following questions to statements that will prompt the speaker to consider your offer to listen to him:

- "Would you like to tell me about it?"
- "Are you willing to talk about it?"
- "Can you tell me what happened?"
- "Is there something you'd like to talk about?"

Today, plan to use an "invitation to talk" with someone you meet. Be sure to carefully observe that person's body language before stating what you observe.

Follow this simple procedure:

1) Observe the nonverbal language of the other person. ("It appears that you're upset.")
2) Offer your "prompt" in statement format. ("I'm here if you want to talk.")
3) Allow for silence. Give the other person time to respond and respect his decision. (Wait quietly for fifteen to twenty seconds.)

Chapter Six

The Process of Reflective Listening

The most important thing in communication is to hear what isn't being said.

—Peter Drucker

Behold, You desire truth in the innermost being.
—Psalm 51:6 (NASB)

Regardless of whether you have used the "invitation to talk" or whether you sense during a casual conversation that the other person has the need to be listened to, the actual reflective listening experience always involves three important components: attending, following, and reflecting. These terms were created by Dr. Robert Bolton in his book *People Skills*.[1]

The important aspects of attending the speaker focus on providing the proper physical setting, being

61

aware of body language, and using soft eye contact as we listen to the speaker. An effective listener also engages in following the speaker as she speaks. Following the speaker includes paying attention to the speaker's body language and using frequent "I'm listening" responses. While attending and following the speaker, reflecting verbally what we think the speaker is attempting to convey must also take place at the appropriate times. Reflecting is the listener's way of enabling both the speaker and herself to focus on the important issues and feelings. If any one of these three components of reflective listening is not present, the effectiveness of the communication will likely be hindered. Here is an in-depth look at each component.

ATTENDING SKILLS

Setting the stage is the first step necessary to any action. In this case, an important aspect of attending the speaker while listening involves providing the proper physical setting. If the setting does not provide for privacy and freedom from distractions, it is recommended that the listener and the speaker move to a more suitable location. Noise and visible distractions must be eliminated to facilitate effective communication.

An example of providing the proper setting occurred the evening Tom stopped by my home to chat. He began the conversation with a casual exchange of information as he stood in my home office. At one point, he mentioned the recent death of a friend.

I quickly noted that the tone of the conversation had changed and sensed that I needed to listen. However, my wife was also in the office working at her computer. The sound of her typing was a distraction to both of us. When I suggested to Tom that we move to the living room, he readily agreed. The private setting away from distractions allowed him to communicate more deeply and with greater ease. It also allowed me to listen more effectively. The fact that we moved from one room to another allowed Tom to get in touch with his true feelings about the death of his friend. As a listener, we should always be aware of the need for privacy.

In addition to providing the proper physical setting for optimum listening results, it is critical that the listener physically attend the one who is speaking. Author M. Scott Peck says: "You cannot truly listen to anyone and do anything else at the same time." We must give the speaker our undivided attention. The three most important aspects of attending include our posture, our gestures, and our eye contact. This is referred to as nonverbal communication. It has been estimated that nonverbal communication accounts for as much as eighty-five percent of all communication.[2] The importance of nonverbal communication cannot be ignored.

Posture is important because it indicates to the speaker whether or not we are willing to listen. To demonstrate a willingness to listen, it is best to be face-to-face with the speaker, leaning slightly toward her while maintaining an open, non-threatening position. Allow the speaker to determine the physical distance that is most comfortable for her, usually somewhere between three to six feet. Someone who leans forward slightly while listening shows a greater interest in what is being said than someone who sits back and puts her hands behind her head. A head movement, such as nodding, or a pensive look conveys a clear message to the speaker that we are attentive to what is being said.

> Listening is a magnetic and strange thing, a creative force. The friends who listen to us are the ones we move toward. When we are listened to, it creates us, makes us unfold and expand.
> —Karl Menninger

Giving the speaker the impression that we are distracted or aren't interested in what is being said will impede the listening process. Crossing the arms often signals that we are not open to what is being said. An example of this is when an umpire crosses his arms when approached by a manager about a questionable call in a baseball game. It is evident to most observers that he doesn't care to listen and isn't planning to change his call. The umpire doesn't have to say a word. His gesture of crossed arms says it all. This example illustrates the power of body language in communicating our feelings to others.

Another important element of attending the speaker is eye contact. We need to maintain soft eye contact, looking gently at the speaker's eyes, nose, hair, shoulders, and face, rather than staring at the eyes or at any other part of the body for an extended period of time. This soft eye contact demonstrates our openness to the speaker and invites more truthful responses from her. Eye contact also allows the listener to hear (see) the deeper meaning that the speaker is attempting to convey. It allows the listener to recognize and take in more than just the words the speaker is saying. Remember, up to eighty-five percent of communication is nonverbal.

On the flip side, we need to be aware not only of our own body language as we attend the speaker, but also of the speaker's body language. As we observe the speaker's body language, we need to watch for clues to her mood and be sensitive to any nervous habits that appear during the listening session. Signs of anxiousness can be detected in facial expressions, as well as in foot, hand, or head movements, such as nervous foot swinging, toe tapping, head shaking and hand wringing. These observations can alert us to the emotional mood of the speaker and provide helpful insights to the issue. It's amazing how quickly subtle body actions can belie the truth of the words we speak.

Never underestimate the importance of providing the proper physical setting and attending the speaker with full-body attention and eye contact. Being aware of and being careful to employ the attending skills will create a positive atmosphere that will encourage the speaker to honestly express her feelings.

FOLLOWING SKILLS

Having addressed the importance of responding nonverbally to the speaker, we can look at the appropriate verbal responses we need to make as the speaker relates what she is thinking. Using "I'm listening" responses throughout the conversation demonstrates that we are following the speaker. Some "I'm listening" phrases and expressions include:

- "Wow!"
- "Uh huh . . ."
- "No kidding!"
- "Great!"
- "Really?"
- "Mmhmm . . ."

It is important to learn to vary the phrases we use while listening reflectively. A listener who repeatedly uses the same word, such as "Really?" or "Wow!" is less convincing about her ability or willingness to follow the speaker. The speaker may suspect that she is not really being heard. The listener who overuses a response may, in fact, discourage and shut the speaker down.

> We believe that how we talk is very important, but we often forget that another aspect—our ability to listen—may be just as important. Good listening is a skill that requires practice, empathy, and true concern for the other person.
>
> —Zig Ziglar

Being careful to vary the "I'm listening" responses can be challenging because it might feel mechanical at first. As listeners, we are trying to motivate the speaker to honestly say what is on her heart. We need to diligently monitor our "I'm listening" responses if we hope to develop effective listening skills. If the "I'm listening" responses are effective, the speaker will be encouraged to express herself more freely.

The third and perhaps most important component of reflective listening is that of verbally reflecting to the speaker what we think she is saying.

REFLECTING SKILLS

Once the speaker has been invited to express her feelings or has touched on an issue during a casual conversation, real listening can begin. A very important component of this real listening is the restatement. This means that we restate what we think the speaker has said. It's a reflection of what we've heard—like holding a mirror up to the conversation. The skill of reflecting can be challenging at first because of the natural tendency to ask questions. To restate what the speaker is trying to say takes concentration.

When we restate what the speaker has said, it is important to precede our restatement with a phrase that will help the speaker understand that we are telling her what we *think* she is saying. Some examples of such phrases are:

- "It sounds like . . ."

- "I sense you . . ."
- "You seem . . ."
- "It appears that . . ."
- "What I hear you saying is . . ."

None of these phrases insinuates to the speaker that we are assuming that we know exactly what she is saying. We are telling her our perception of what she is saying. Memorizing these phrases will keep us from developing a habit of using only one or two of them. This is very helpful as we gain confidence in reflecting what the speaker says.

This part of the reflective process can be tiring at first, but practicing this step will enable us to listen and reflect with increasing ease. If we want to become a reflective listener, it is important that we master the skill of restating or reflecting what the speaker says. Reflecting is the oil that lubricates the conversation. This is where both we and the speaker will find out if we've really been listening or not.

It is important to restate what we think we have heard in words other than what the speaker used. The following interaction illustrates how to restate what the speaker says.

Dan: "Harvey is mean and he makes me feel stupid!"

Ryan: "It sounds like Harvey upsets you."

Ryan's statement validates that Dan must have a reason for calling Harvey mean. Let's take that same statement and react to it in another way:

Dan: "Harvey is mean and he makes me feel stupid!"

Ryan: "I sense that you don't like the way Harvey treats you."

People sometimes ask, "What if neither statement is accurate?" If this is the case, the speaker will correct the listener's misconception. What is most important is that the listener has demonstrated a willingness to listen.

We must remember that the restatement is our wording of what we think the other person is saying. The following example illustrates how to restate what the speaker is attempting to say:

Joe: "I can't wait until this class is over!" (*comment*)

Bob: "It sounds like you're not enjoying the class." (*restatement*)

Joe: "No, it's not that. I really like it." (*clarification*)

Bob: "So what you're saying is that you *are* enjoying the class." (*restatement*)

Joe: "Yes! But I can't wait till it's over so I can use what I've learned!"

Bob's initial restatement of what he thought Joe was saying was not accurate. When Bob restated what he thought Joe was saying, it gave Joe the chance to correct him. Joe knew that Bob was actively listening. He then adjusted his comment to give Bob a clearer idea of what he meant to say. Bob's second restatement was more accurate. It also motivated Joe to say more about his reason for wanting to complete the course.

A typical conversation such as this might occur between a parent and a teenage son:

Son: "The coach always yells at me during practice. Whenever I do something wrong he gets in my face."

Parent: "So you're saying that the coach gets upset with you."

Son: "You said it! Tonight when we ran the first play, I blocked the guy across the line from me and the coach yelled at me and told me I was supposed to block the guy next to him. He said I hit the wrong guy."

Parent: "It sounds like the coach wasn't happy that you blocked the wrong guy."

Son: "Yeah!"

Note that the parent in this conversation conveyed an open and accepting attitude by restating what she thought her son was trying to communicate.

This is one of the most critical values of the restatement—it prevents the listener from falling into the trap of reverting to any one of the communication stumbling blocks. The parent in this exchange did not question, judge, advise, or reassure her son.

The restatement focuses on the speaker. It gives us the opportunity to let the speaker know that we are sincerely listening to her. It is very important to practice restating what others say to us. We can practice these restatements when interacting with strangers such as the grocery store cashier or the restaurant server. It gives valuable practice and makes other people feel good to know that someone—even a passing stranger—is listening to them.

> When you are listening to somebody, completely, attentively, then you are listening not only to the words, but also to the feeling of what is being conveyed, to the whole of it, not part of it.
> —Jiddu Krishnamurti

It is not necessary to restate or reflect every single statement made by the speaker. Doing so may be perceived as condescending and insulting. A listener who is over-zealous in reflecting may act in the following way:

Jon (speaker): "I'm having a problem with my computer."

Bill (listener): "It sounds like your computer is giving you problems."

Jon: "It started to make a weird sound last night."

Bill: "So it's sounding weird."

Jon: "I turned it off . . ."

Bill (interrupting to reflect): "You're telling me that you turned it off."

Jon (looking irritated because he is being interrupted by Bill's insistence on reflecting every single statement he makes): "I turned it off and unplugged it three times."

Bill (quickly interrupting to reflect again): "I hear you saying that you turned it off three times."

Jon (deciding to stop the conversation, looks at his watch): "Boy, I really have to run. I'm going to be late for an appointment."

What happened here? Instead of giving Jon the opportunity to explain, Bill attempted to reflect every statement Jon made. When this occurs, the focus shifts to the listener rather than staying on the issue the speaker is attempting to present. Reflecting too frequently in a conversation prevents the speaker from talking.

REFLECTING FACTS AND FEELINGS

As listeners, we have the choice to reflect either the facts that are presented to us or the speaker's feelings. Reflecting facts is less challenging and often the safest response. We simply restate what we hear the speaker say. The following conversation between Ruth and Ann is an example of reflecting facts.

Ruth calls from her front porch to her neighbor Ann: "Guess what? My daughter Rose and the grandkids are coming to stay with us for a whole month this summer!" Ann's reflection of the facts could be, "So you're saying that Rose and her kids will be visiting you for four weeks this summer."

The more challenging reflective statement focuses on the speaker's feelings. Reflecting feelings is more subjective and requires an astute observation of the speaker's body language and tone of voice.

Since feelings are sensitive, reflecting a person's feelings must be done with caution. Several factors are involved in our comfort with reflecting the speaker's feelings: the relationship that exists between us and the speaker, the amount of trust between us and speaker, and the depth of the issue presented.

Let's revisit the conversation between Ruth and Ann. This time Ann is going to reflect what she believes are Ruth's feelings about the situation. Ruth has just told Ann "Guess what?! My daughter Rose and the grandkids are coming to stay with us for a whole month this summer!" Ann, noting Ruth's facial and vocal expression, says, "I can tell you're really excited about Rose's visit!" She might also say "It sounds like you're really looking forward to this summer." Either reflection focuses on and validates Ruth's feelings.

By reflecting the speaker's feelings, we encourage the speaker to move beyond the facts and acknowledge any underlying emotions or issues.

SUMMARIZING

Another very important component of reflecting skills is summarizing. When people find someone who will listen to them, they tend to unload a lot of information. When listening to a person "gush," we should try to focus on just a few of the important facts or feelings that have been expressed. Often the speaker will mention a certain situation or a particular emotion several times. She might also emphasize a situation with a great deal of intensity. Any time the speaker revisits an event or an emotion during the course of the conversation, a red flag should go up in our minds. This serves as a cue and should alert us to the possibility that here is something we should focus on when reflecting back to the speaker. Remember to respond frequently with the "I'm listening" responses.

Even the most skilled listener can handle only so much information and emotion at one time. We've been taught that it is impolite to interrupt. However, when a person is overwhelming us with information or emotion, there are three reasons why we must interrupt her. First, we will not be able to continue listening if the speaker is allowed to continue gushing. This is because we have reached our information saturation level. Second, it will give us the opportunity to clarify what we believe the person has revealed. Third, the speaker needs someone to help her focus and sort through the facts and her feelings. By interrupting the speaker with these intentions, we are actually demonstrating that we care enough to listen well.

When interrupting the speaker, it is important to be polite. Treat the speaker with respect. Summarizing statements such as the following might be appropriate after listening to the speaker gush for several minutes:

- "You stated four times that . . ."

- "An emotion that I sense you were feeling as you talked was . . ."
- "A number of times I heard you mention . . ."
- "The main theme you keep coming back to is . . ."
- "Your focus seems to be . . ."

Summarizing is extremely important to the flow of a conversation when the speaker has a lot to say. It becomes cumbersome if we attempt to interrupt every statement the speaker makes with a reflection or a summary. We must get out of the way so the speaker can talk. We have to decide how much information we can handle before interrupting the speaker. One person may be able to listen to a lot of information before interrupting while another person might feel compelled to interrupt more frequently. Usually the more skilled we become at listening, the more information we can handle before interrupting the speaker.

Two people listening to the same conversation may select two different issues to summarize. Neither one is wrong. Each listener will summarize or react to what she thinks the speaker is attempting to communicate. Again, the most important matter is that the speaker is being listened to. If we have missed the real issue, repeatedly listening, restating, and summarizing will enable the speaker to eventually arrive at her real concern.

BE AS HONEST AS POSSIBLE

Listeners need to be as honest as possible. There may be times we need to interrupt a speaker and say, "I am confused about . . . ." This lets the speaker know that we are listening. She will be encouraged by our caring attitude and eager to clarify the issue and continue sharing. An important point to remember is that we must demonstrate to the speaker that we are trying to listen to her. We must not get frustrated if we don't reflect accurately the first, second, or third time. The speaker may not actually be stating the facts or her feelings clearly. This may be the case when strong emotion is present. We can reflect only the information the speaker gives us. The beauty of reflective listening is that the listener—by reflecting the speaker's words—enables the speaker to clearly and effectively express herself.

In our scenarios, Brenda is preparing to listen to Julie who has just come home from school.

Brenda: "Hi, Sweetheart. It looks like something's bothering you. I'm here if you want to talk about it." She allows time for Julie to react and, as Julie is thinking, Brenda stops what she is doing and sits down at the kitchen table so she can give Julie her full attention. She is determined to respect whatever Julie says.

Julie: "Yeah, Emily told me I was stupid because I failed the math quiz this morning. I forgot we were having the quiz. There were a lot of other kids in the class who failed it too. Even Emily didn't do so well herself—she got a C+."

Brenda nods to indicate she is listening. She focuses on her daughter as Julie vents her feelings, and then says, "Mmhmm."

Julie: "Emily really bugs me!"

Brenda: "It sounds like she made fun of you."

Julie: "Emily makes fun of me all the time. Mom, she makes fun of a lot of kids. She's so mean. She's really not a good friend. She acts like she's so much better than everyone else and I'm tired of it."

Brenda: "I get the impression that you don't like the way Emily treats you."

Brenda is doing a terrific job of reflecting as she listens to Julie.

In the next scenario, Mike picks up his son Kyle at school. Kyle climbs into the passenger seat looking thoughtful.

Mike: "It looks as if you've got a lot on your mind. I'd be interested in hearing about it." He turns the ignition off and shifts in the driver's seat to face Kyle, as he gives his son time to consider the invitation.

Kyle (after a few moments): "Larry says he's going to join the Air Force after we graduate. Dad, do you think I should go to college or join the Air Force?"

Mike: "It sounds like you're not sure what to do." (Note that Mike does not answer Kyle's question.)

Kyle: "I thought I wanted to go to college, but joining the Air Force with Larry sounds like a cool idea. Four of the guys said they are thinking of joining with Larry. Boy, it would be great if we could all go together!"

Mike, who is shocked by what Kyle has just said, sits in silence with his son.

In the third scenario Faith is dealing with Jerry's angry look.

Faith: "It looks like you're upset, Hon. I'm willing to listen." Faith stops what she is doing and turns to face Jerry as she gives him time to decide how to respond to her invitation.

Jerry: "My boss told me I'm not doing a good job. He should talk. I have to clean up his messes all the time!"

Faith: "That must have been a pretty hard blow."

Jerry nods in agreement.

Fourth is the scenario with Steph and Diane. Diane has just told Steph that her daughter Jessica has been picking on a girl in her class. Steph realizes that the grocery store is not a good place to discuss such a sensitive subject, so she asks Diane to call her later so they can get together to talk. At 9:00 p.m., Diane calls to tell Steph that she can talk now since the kids are in bed. Steph drives across town to Diane's home to listen. (Listening reflectively is not always convenient.)

Since Steph and Diane have relocated to an environment more conducive to listening, Steph is able to effectively resume the conversation with an invitation to talk.

Steph: "You mentioned earlier today that Jessica was picking on a girl at school. I'd like to hear more about that."

Diane: "Oh, Steph, I don't know what to do. I've talked to Jessica and she told me that the other girl always calls her names. When she asks her to stop it, that girl tells the teacher that Jessica is trying to pick a fight with her."

Steph nods and says, "Mmmm."

Diane: "I never dreamed my daughter would be accused of picking a fight. She doesn't even pick on Josh or Emma at home. She's always been a big help to me. It just doesn't make sense that she would pick on someone at school."

Steph: "I can tell that this is really bothering you."

Diane sits motionless as tears stream down her cheeks. Because Steph listened reflectively, Diane felt comfortable and was able to open up to her.

We now join Kevin and Zach, who are having breakfast at Kelly's Café. Kevin initiates the conversation by inviting Zach to continue where they left off the last time they were together.

Kevin: "The last time we talked, you mentioned that you felt your secretary was not doing her job. I'm interested in hearing how that's going."

Kevin does not begin with a question. He focuses on an important issue that Zach had presented during their previous conversation. This opens the door for Zack to talk about it if he feels comfortable doing so. Kevin gives Zach time to consider the invitation.

Zach: "I don't know what to do. Patti had great recommendations and she dresses professionally. Her typing is good, but she has a hard time keeping up with the books."

Kevin needs clarification: "I'm not sure exactly what you mean when you say she has a hard time keeping up with the books."

"Well . . ." Zach hesitates. "Well . . . there were just a few times when she didn't enter the information when I thought she should have."

Kevin: "So that's what frustrates you most—the fact that she's not doing things as quickly as you'd like her to."

Zach: "Well, she's actually not doing that badly, but I keep giving her suggestions about how to run the office and she hasn't followed through on any of them . . . ."

Kevin continues to follow Zach as he concentrates on Zach's words and posture.

Kevin: "I sense that you're not sure how to handle this."

Zach nods in agreement.

We can see that all of our listeners are doing their jobs. They are attending, following, and reflecting. Each of our listeners was prepared for whatever the speaker would say. Just as we would not wait to prepare for a crisis until it arrives (of course by then it's too late!), we also need to know how to listen reflectively and be skilled and comfortable in carrying it out before a critical situation is on our doorstep. By practicing daily in nonthreatening, noncrisis situations, we will be able to effectively handle ourselves at a time when it becomes extremely crucial to employ effective communication skills.

Something to think about . . .

Here are actions you can take:
Tell a friend that you want to practice your listening skills. Ask him or her to present a hypothetical or real situation.

- Practice the "I'm listening" comments and gestures ("uh huh," "right," nod your head, etc.)
- Practice making reflective statements ("So what you're saying is . . ." "I sense that . . ." "It sounds like . . ." etc.)
- Practice summarizing what is being said ("Four times you mentioned . . ." "You seem to be focused on . . ." "I keep hearing you say . . .," etc.)

Another suggestion:

- The next time you go to the local supermarket or store, use an "invitation to talk" with the cashier ("You look cheerful," "It looks like you are really busy today," "I'll bet you're eager for your shift to end," "You seem to enjoy your job," etc.). Refrain from using a question.

- Reflect back to that person what you think she is saying. This will provide practice with little emotional involvement. (Note: I really enjoy listening to strangers at the local stores. It makes my day and, hopefully, it makes the day a little better for each person I take the time to listen to as well!)

Chapter Seven

Silence Is Golden

Under all speech that is good for anything there lies a silence that is better. Silence is deep as Eternity; speech is shallow as Time.

—Thomas Carlyle

Those who control their tongue will have a long life; opening your mouth can ruin everything.

—Proverbs 13:3

Silence is an important nonverbal component of effective listening. Periods of silence throughout the conversation are very beneficial to both the speaker and the listener. Although few people are comfortable with silence in a conversation, it is extremely vital to the speaker for two reasons. One, it allows the speaker to reflect on what he has said. Two, silence provides encouragement to the speaker by giving him time and space to experience his feelings. It will often serve as a gentle nudge for him to go deeper into the conversation.

Silence is also beneficial to the listener. During a period of silence, the listener is very busy. Silence allows the listener to attend the speaker, to observe the speaker, to think about what the speaker might be feeling, and, most importantly, to pray for wisdom as he listens.

As listeners, we must become comfortable with whatever period of silence the speaker allows without trying to fill it with words. A skilled listener will discipline himself to focus on the speaker during times of silence. Using this time to observe the speaker's nonverbal communication gives the listener a greater understanding of the emotions the speaker is experiencing.

Often the quickest change of direction in the course of conversation occurs after a period of silence. We need to be prepared for the speaker to respond to the silence in one of several ways—displaying anxiety, asking to discontinue the conversation, sharing a startling insight, or taking the conversation in a completely different direction.

> Well-timed silence hath more eloquence than speech.
>
> —Martin Fraguhar Tupper

We must be comfortable with periods of silence before we can be effective as reflective listeners.

However, periods of silence that exceed forty-five seconds can hinder effective communication.

If the speaker remains silent for a long period of time, we might need to end the silence. Ending the silence can be done in one of three ways: 1) We can give the speaker permission to stop, 2) We can state our observation of what we sense he is feeling, or 3) We can summarize what we've heard him say. Any of these responses to the speaker's silence will encourage the speaker to either stop or resume the conversation. Whatever we do, we keep our focus on the speaker. We do not use silence to shift the focus to ourselves.

To illustrate how vital silence is during a conversation, here is an experience I had many years ago. During a demonstration for a communication skills class, I listened to Cindy. At one point in the conversation, there was a significant period of silence during which Cindy appeared to be deep in thought. Tears welled up in her eyes and she began to gently wring her hands and stare at the floor. During this sensitive moment, I realized that she had gotten in touch with a deep emotion. I whispered her name and said, "We can stop if you want to." She nodded her head and looked at me with a sense of relief as we ended the session. Being aware of her body language during the silence enabled me to sense the emotional turmoil she was experiencing. Giving Cindy permission to stop the conversation was a demonstration of my sensitivity and respect for her as a speaker.

> Remember not only to say the right thing in the right place but, far more difficult still, to leave unsaid the wrong thing at the tempting moment.
>
> —Ben Franklin

Let's look again at each of the listening scenarios to see how the listeners handle silence. Note the change of direction that each conversation takes as a result of the period of silence.

Julie has told her mother that she is tired of Emily making fun of her all the time. Brenda's last comment was "I get the impression that you don't like the way Emily treats you." Julie hangs her head and sighs. Tears begin to well up in her eyes as her mother sits quietly with her. Many things are going through Brenda's mind as she watches her daughter struggle with her emotions. Finally, after what seems like a long period of silence, Julie looks at her mother and asks, "Mom, do you think I'm stupid?"

Kyle has just told his dad that he is thinking of joining the Air Force rather than going to college. Kyle's last statement was "I thought I wanted to go to college, but joining the Air Force with Larry sounds like a cool idea. Four of the other guys said they are thinking of joining with Larry. Boy, it would be great if we could all go together!" This is a shock to Mike as he sits in silence with his son. After several moments, Kyle finally breaks the silence with, "Dad, what do you think I should do?"

Now Mike has a decision to make, answer the question or turn the question back to Kyle.

Jerry has just told Faith that his boss doesn't think he is doing a good job. Jerry's statement has surprised Faith, but she remains focused on listening. Her reaction to Jerry's comment is "That must have been a pretty hard blow."

Jerry nods in agreement and then is silent for a long period of time. Faith can see that he is fighting back tears. He shakes his head in disbelief. Finally, he looks up at Faith questioningly and says, "You're acting strange."

Faith: "I'm not sure what you mean."

Jerry responds, "Well . . ., you usually pump me with questions, but today you're quiet and just looking at me. I'm not used to that."

Faith takes some time before responding. She decides to be honest. "It sounds like you're uncomfortable with how I'm responding."

Jerry: "Well, it's different. I'm just not used to it."

Faith: "The seminar I attended at church last weekend was about becoming a better listener. The Lord showed me that I have been a very poor listener for many years. I realize now that it's not good to ask questions. I knew it bothered you, but I didn't know what else to do. Now I have a better idea of how to listen. From now on, I'm going to do my best to listen to you. Jerry, I love you and I want to be the best wife that I can be." She pauses and waits silently before continuing. "You said that your boss told you that you're not doing a good job. I can't imagine how that must have made you feel."

Jerry: "Wow! You really do care about my feelings." He pauses. "Actually, I'd have to agree with my boss—my heart just hasn't been in it lately."

Jerry stops and a long period of silence follows. Finally, he looks at Faith and blurts, "What would you say if I told you I wanted to quit my job?"

How will Faith respond to Jerry's question?

It is important at this time that we address Jerry's reaction to Faith as she listens reflectively. He is accustomed to being bombarded with questions and the unexpected change in Faith's approach to communication confuses him.

A few months after I began using reflective listening skills, a friend and I were engaged in a casual conversation. He mentioned a particular issue a number of times and I realized that I needed to listen reflectively. I began to reflect as he talked openly about what was bothering him. Suddenly, he paused and asked, "What's different about you?" After a period of silence, my response was "I'm not sure what you mean." He replied, "You usually ask a lot of questions and talk about yourself." His reaction shocked me. It had never occurred to me that he had been conditioned to have me respond with frequent questions and self-editorializing. I told him that I realized I had been a poor listener and that I was working on becoming a better listener. He nodded his head and I listened as he continued to share. The experience of people questioning my new approach was repeated numerous times during the first year that I began to listen reflectively.

When we become reflective listeners, it is not uncommon for relatives and friends to have the same reaction as my friend and as Jerry did in this scenario. As we consistently demonstrate our willingness to listen, others will grow to appreciate that we are sincerely listening to them.

In an earlier scenario, Steph is in Diane's kitchen as Diane processes the fact that her daughter Jessica is being accused of bullying a girl at school. Steph's comment is "I can tell that this is really bothering you."

Diane: "Steph, my daughter isn't a bully! I know she's not perfect, but she doesn't pick on other kids. This other girl has a reputation for getting kids in trouble. I called her teacher and told her that I don't believe that my daughter is the one causing the problem. Well, the teacher proceeded to tell me that she has caught Jessica yelling at the other girl several times. Now, my husband is upset with me because I didn't tell him about the situation sooner. He accuses me of never letting him know what's going on with the kids." Diane hangs her head and weeps silently.

Steph: "Wow, you do have a lot on your plate right now."

Diane looks up at Steph after a period of silence and asks, "Steph, how can I keep Jim from getting mad at me all the time?"

This is not the direction Steph thought the conversation would go. Now she will have to handle this sudden turn.

As we can see, listening reflectively really has the power to reveal the truth. In the conversation between Kevin and Zach, Zach appears to be at the point where he doesn't know how to tell his secretary, Patti, that she needs to do better with the bookkeeping. Kevin's last reflection was, "I sense that you're not sure how to handle this."

Kevin sits quietly as Zack contemplates his next statement. He notices that Zach seems to be dealing with inner turmoil. He is ready to tell Zach that they do not have to continue when Zach looks Kevin in the eye and asks, "Kevin, have you ever struggled with being attracted to another woman? I mean, like she's always on your mind and you want to be with her all the time? Kevin, you've gotta believe me, bro—I love my wife, but I'm scared to death by how I'm starting to feel toward Patti! What am I going to do?"

Kevin did not expect to hear that. They have been friends for many years. Zach is married and has three children. Kevin's recovery from shock requires another important skill in reflective listening—what to do when the speaker asks a question.

Something to think about . . .

While continuing to practice the skills that were introduced in Chapter 6, focus also on allowing silence. Practice becoming comfortable with silence—even seemingly long periods of silence—in your everyday conversations. Consciously and silently count slowly to ten or fifteen for starters. As you become comfortable with that much silence, increase your count to thirty. Allow the other person to be the first to break the silence.

Chapter Eight

Handling Questions Presented by the Speaker

To listen closely and reply well is the highest perfection we are able to attain in the art of conversation.

—Francois de La Rochefoucauld

The heart of the godly thinks carefully before speaking.

—Proverbs 15:28a

As a speaker demonstrates the need to work through issues, it is not uncommon for her to ask a question. Herein lies one of the most difficult aspects of reflective listening—refraining from answering questions. Some listeners think, "What do you mean—'don't answer the question!' She asked the question because she wanted an answer, right?" Not necessarily. As contrary to human reasoning as it may seem, we must not assume that a person who asks a question expects us to answer. A skilled listener is free from the responsibility of answering or resolving the speaker's problem. Therefore, the listener need not feel compelled to answer questions presented by the speaker.

Why do people ask questions if they don't want an answer? This is one of the many mysteries of communication. Questions seem to be a safe way for a speaker to find out if we are willing to listen. But when we refrain from answering a speaker's question, we will usually discover that she has more to say and, when given the opportunity to do so, will often answer her own question. We must never assume that we have the answer to the speaker's question. A speaker will often introduce a "presenting problem" before getting to the real issue. Therefore, it is usually not wise or helpful to answer the question that is initially presented.

How Not to Answer Questions

What should the listener do when asked a question? There are several different ways to respond without answering the question—all of them equally appropriate and productive. The first option is to reflect back to the speaker—in statement format—what we have heard her say. For instance, if the speaker asks, "What do you think I should do?" we could respond by saying "It sounds like you're not sure what to do." I call this type of response REFLECTING the question.

The second option in responding to a question is called DEFLECTING. When deflecting, the listener essentially changes the speaker's question into a statement and passes it back to the speaker for her to respond. Deflecting a question gives us the opportunity to let the speaker know that the most important thing is not how we feel, but how she feels. If asked, "What do you think I should do?" the listener could respond with "Right now, I'm more interested in what *you* think you should do." Many times after a question has been deflected, the speaker quickly begins to offer more information. As we attentively watch and listen, she will usually answer her own question.

A third alternative to answering a question presented by the speaker is INSPECTING. This occurs when the listener invites the speaker to provide more information. The listener's response to the question, "What do you think I should do?" could be "I'd like to hear some of the things that you've already done." This is a very non-threatening way of seeking more information without asking a question.

A fourth alternative to answering the speaker's question is to not respond to the question at all. This is called IGNORING the question. Ignoring a question is often the best option when the speaker is sharing a lot of information in the midst of the listening experience. When we respond to a question with silence, it gives the speaker time to think and often she will begin to give her own response even though we did not solicit it. Remaining silent and waiting a few seconds after the speaker asks a question will often cause her to continue with the conversation and answer her own question.

We need to be extremely cautious about answering the speaker's questions for two basic reasons:

1) We may not have the answer.
2) Even if we think we know the answer, is what the speaker is asking really the problem?

Regardless of which option is used, when we do not answer the speaker's question, it encourages her to continue. We are allowing her the freedom to discover the answer to her own question. Since we do not necessarily have the answer for her, it is better to listen well and watch the speaker solve her own problem.

THREE PERSONAL EXAMPLES OF NOT ANSWERING

One evening while dining in a restaurant with two other couples, the gentleman next to me asked, "Dick, have you ever taken any counseling courses?" I started to answer his question, but quickly realized by his body language—a blank stare and the absence of head nods in response to what I was saying—that he did not want an answer. So I said, "I'm interested in why you'd like to know that." His reply was, "My wife has taken several counseling courses, and I'm wondering if I should take some courses as well."

Note that he had not yet expressed what was really bothering him. Knowingly or unknowingly, he was using the initial question to determine if I would really listen to him. At this point, I began to reflect what he was saying and within a few minutes he began to talk about his frustration with someone whom he was attempting to counsel. I was able to listen and help him process some of his concerns. If I had continued to respond to his original question, I would have dominated the conversation and given him an answer that was really not important to him.

On another occasion, I was riding in the car with Todd when he began to speak about a concern he had about his future. It wasn't long before he asked, "Dick, what do you think I should do?" I looked at him and honestly said, "You know that I teach people how to listen. One thing I teach in the seminars is not to answer questions. I'm going to practice what I teach and I'm going to tell you that I don't have an answer for you. However, I'm interested in what you've already considered." I watched with excitement as Todd revealed without hesitation the options he had thought of as well as the advice that he had received from other people. My lack of response prompted him to continue to express his own thoughts and to go deeper into his concern. Forty-five minutes later, he had revealed more options than I could've given him. During the conversation, he asked me at least four times what I thought he should do. I never gave him an answer because I didn't know what he should do. I firmly believe that it's not my responsibility to solve problems for others. By the way, Todd did solve the problem for himself by the time that conversation had ended.

During a conversation with Kara, she insisted five times that I give her advice about an issue she was struggling with. I knew that I did not have the answer for her and I wasn't confident that the issue she was presenting was the real issue. After asking for my advice the fifth time—and after I had either reflected, deflected, inspected, or ignored her request each of those five times—the conversation moved to a deeper level and in a completely different direction. The first problem she had presented was the presenting problem. Some people will test us thoroughly before they trust our ability or willingness to listen rather than give advice, ask questions, or offer reassurance. If I had given Kara advice about the presenting problem, it's very likely that she never would have arrived at the real issue.

Each person has the ability to find the answer to her own situation or problem. Our task is to be there and to listen to the other person—reflecting what she says and validating her feelings. In essence, my job as a listener is to reflect some of the important things that the speaker has told me.

PRESENTING ISSUE OR REAL ISSUE

People who give advice too quickly often give advice about the presenting issue rather than the real issue.

Handling Questions Presented
by the Speaker

A reflective listener is patient and allows the speaker to wade through the issue until she arrives at the real problem.

But what if the speaker really does want us to answer her question? If this is true, the person asking the question will often restate it several times so we will know that she really does want a response from us. And we may feel free to give advice (although it's always wise to be cautious in this area) only after we are absolutely certain that that is what she wants and that the real issue is at hand.

We should ask ourselves, "Does she really want me to answer or should I reflect this question back to her to find out what is really on her mind?" When we are unsure, it is always best—and will often produce surprising results—to use reflecting skills.

In the scenarios used before, each listener has been presented with a challenging question.

Julie asks Brenda, "Mom, do you think I'm stupid?"

Brenda wants so badly to reassure her daughter. It is not easy to be with someone who is struggling without attempting to make her feel better. Brenda quickly decides to pass the question back to Julie.

Brenda: "Julie, what's more important to me is whether you feel that you're stupid."

Julie: "Mr. Kelp, my math teacher, keeps telling me that I'm not good at math. He made fun of me in class yesterday for having a problem wrong on my homework assignment. One other time, I was so embarrassed that I wanted to walk out of class. Mom, he treats me as if I don't know anything! I have a "C" right now, no thanks to him. Once, I got a "D" on a test and when I asked him what I did wrong on a few of the problems, he just laughed and told me I made stupid mistakes."

Brenda: "You're saying that Mr. Kelp humiliates you."

Julie: "Yeah! He makes fun of me in front of the whole class. I'm afraid to ask any questions. If I can't talk to the teacher without him making fun of me, how am I supposed to get any help?"

Again, Brenda does not answer Julie's question.

Brenda: "Julie, tell me some of the things you have thought of."

Julie: "Well . . ., I've thought about going to the guidance counselor, Ms. Ramsey. Mary told me Mrs. Sleden was picking on her and Ms. Ramsey helped her. I even thought about going to Mr. Black, the assistant principal, but I'm not sure if I want to do that."

Brenda: "It sounds like you've considered several different ways to handle the situation."

Julie: "Yeah, I have, but I'm afraid Mr. Kelp will get worse if I talk to Ms. Ramsey or Mr. Black because I know they'll tell him what I say . . . and I'm afraid he'll take it out on me."

Brenda: "I sense that you're really struggling with this."

Julie: "Mom, what should I do? I hate math and I hate Mr. Kelp!"

Brenda is struggling with her own emotions. By answering Julie's question, she would be giving advice and controlling the conversation. She's also not convinced that this is the real problem. She knows that she needs to listen to her daughter so she decides not to answer the question and waits silently while her daughter ponders her dilemma.

Julie, after a long period of silence, says, "Mom, Mary said she'd go with me to see Ms. Ramsey and I think I'm gonna take her up on that offer. I'm gonna see if we can meet with her tomorrow during study hall."

Brenda: "You seem pretty determined that that's what you're going to do."

Julie: "Yup . . . I think it's the best thing. I think I'll go see Ms. Ramsey tomorrow."

In the next scenario, Kyle has just asked, "Dad, what do you think I should do, go to college or join the Air Force?"

Mike: "Kyle, I'd like to hear more about what you're thinking."

Kyle: "Boy, Larry is set on joining the Air Force. He's been bugging me for weeks about signing up with him. I don't want him to get mad at me."

Mike: "It sounds like you're really concerned about what Larry thinks."

Kyle, after several moments of silence: "You know what, Dad? It's my life and I think I'd like to be a teacher." He pauses again before continuing. "I don't care if Larry does get mad at me—I'm gonna go to college and do what I wanna do!"

Mike: "I have a feeling you really mean that."

Kyle: "I do, Dad. I really do. And, hey, thanks a lot for listening."

Because Mike took the time to listen to Kyle and help him process his thoughts and feelings without judging, questioning, or advising him, Kyle is able to focus on what he really wants to do.

In the Faith and Jerry scenario, Jerry has just shocked Faith with a question she never expected. He wants to know how she would feel if he quit his job.

Faith: "Wow! So you're thinking about quitting your job." The couple falls into a silent gaze as Faith waits for Jerry to continue.

Jerry: "I've been struggling with something for several months." He pauses. "I feel called to be a pastor. I know it probably sounds crazy to think about going back to school at my age, but lately it's all I can think about."

Faith gives herself time before she reflects. Then she says, "What I hear you saying is that you believe God is calling you into the ministry."

Jerry: "Yeah! Crazy, isn't it?"

Faith: "Well, it seems as if you've really given it a lot of thought."

Jerry: "You're right. I've looked into a number of seminaries and the one I'm interested in is near Mom and Dad. What would you think about living with them for a few months until we could find a place of our own?"

Faith: "You really have thought this through!"

Jerry: "Yeah, I have."

What a twist that listening experience took.

Now, checking in with Steph and Diane, we see that Diane was presenting a problem about her daughter Jessica being accused of bullying in school. But now Diane has taken a complete turn to the issue of her husband, Jim, being angry with her. Diane's question to Steph is, "How can I keep Jim from being mad at me all the time?"

Steph: "It sounds to me as if you feel that Jim gets upset with you quite a bit." There is a long period of silence as Diane tries unsuccessfully to fight back tears.

Diane, now sobbing, whispers, "Jim told me yesterday that he doesn't love me anymore and that he wants a divorce . . . . Oh, Steph! What am I gonna do?"

Steph is silent for a long time before she responds in a soft voice of disbelief, "You're telling me that Jim wants a divorce."

Diane: "Yeah . . . . Our marriage has been on the rocks for a long time, but I was hoping we could work things out. I never thought it would come to this."

Both women sit in silence for several moments. Steph's thoughts are racing as she struggles with how to best respond to this shocking news. After several minutes, Diane looks at Steph and says, "You're the first person I've told."

Steph: "Oh, Diane, I had no idea that things were so rough."

Diane: "It feels so good to finally tell someone."

Steph: "Diane, you and Jim will be in my prayers. And anytime you need to talk, don't hesitate to call me."

In the last scenario, Kevin and Zach are still at the restaurant where Zach has just dropped a bomb on Kevin by asking, "Have you ever struggled with being attracted to another woman? I mean, like she's always on your mind and you want to be with her all the time? Kevin, you've gotta believe me, bro—I love my wife, but I'm scared to death by how I'm starting to feel toward Patti! What am I going to do?"

Kevin takes a lot of time before speaking as he observes his friend drop his head in shame. "You're telling me that you're attracted to Patti."

Zach: "Yeah. It's something I never expected to happen. I think it started when I asked her to stay late a few times and then we'd grab a bite to eat afterwards. Kevin, I can't go on like this! I don't want to hurt my wife or ruin my marriage. What can I do?"

Kevin: "Right now I'm more interested in what you think you should do."

Zach, after a long silence: "Kevin, I've thought about this a lot . . . and the only thing that's going to work is if I ask Patti to resign."

Kevin: "Wow."

Zach: "Yeah . . . I'm going to have to talk to her tomorrow. I can't let this go on any longer."

Kevin: "It sounds like you've decided that that's the best solution."

Zach: "Yeah. It's going to be tough, but I know it's what I have to do."

Kevin: "You know I'll be praying for you."

Zach: "Thanks . . . . And thanks for listening, too." After a period of silence, he continues. "Hey, I was wondering if we could get together every so often. I really need to be accountable to someone."

Kevin: "You bet! How about if we meet here again next Saturday morning at 9:00?"

Zach: "That would be great."

Kevin: "OK. I'll see you next Saturday. Give me a call before then if you need to talk."

Zach: "Thanks, Kevin. I don't know what I'd do if I had to deal with this alone."

Kevin: "Hey . . . that's what friends are for!"

Each of the listeners in these scenarios was an extension of God's love to someone who was hurting. Julie, Kyle, Jerry, Diane, and Zach are no different from the rest of us. They have struggles, as we all do. They all needed one thing—a friend who could and would listen. Will we be that friend to those around us who are struggling?

LISTENING TO A POSITIVE EXPERIENCE

Though the emphasis of the scenarios has dealt frequently with individuals who were experiencing a difficult situation, it is just as important to listen to someone who is excited about a positive experience.

Most people look for others who will help them celebrate a joyous event or share their happiness. This provides the listener with an easier listening experience since most pleasant situations do not come with a hidden agenda.

Here are several listening experiences based on positive situations. Watch how the listeners reflect to let the speaker know that he or she is being heard.

Billy is a second grader. At the end of the day, he gets off the bus and runs up the sidewalk to his front porch. His mother, Twila, sees him coming. The big smile on his face indicates that something exciting must have happened.

Billy: "Hey, Mom! Guess what? I kicked the ball in gym today!"

Twila: "You're saying you kicked the ball. Wow!"

Billy: "Yeah, Michael was on third and I brought him home. We won 2-1."

Twila: "You won!"

Billy: "Yeah!"

Twila: "That must feel really great."

Billy: "Yeah! Hey, can I have some cookies?"

Twila stayed focused on Billy as he related the incident. In the end, she was able to identify and validate his feelings about hitting the home run. Once Billy was satisfied that he had been heard and that his joy had been shared, he ran off to something else.

In the second scenario, Brooke, a kindergarten student, approaches her teacher during recess one morning in May to tell her some exciting news.

Handling Questions Presented by the Speaker

Brooke: "Mrs. Varner, my mommy's gonna have a baby."

Mrs. Varner: "Your mommy is going to have a baby."

Brooke: "Yeah, she says he's coming in September."

Mrs. Varner: "He's coming in September."

Brooke: "Yup. We're gonna call him Seth."

Mrs. Varner: "You're going to call him Seth."

Brooke: "Yeah. I can't wait." She then turns and runs off to play.

One important point about Mrs. Varner's reflective statements as she listens to Brooke is that she is very careful to reflect back to Brooke using the same words that Brooke used. Reflecting the exact words of younger children is important because we want them to understand that we are hearing exactly what they are saying. Robert Bolton refers to this as "parroting."[1]

Parroting usually works well with young children up to the age of nine or ten. By that age, most children have developed a vocabulary that enables them to understand when we reflect the essence of what they have said rather than simply parroting their words.

Here is a conversation between Riley, a first grader, and her teacher, Mrs. Smith. It is more negative than positive but shows parroting. Riley enters the classroom after getting off the bus. Her expression indicates that something is bothering her. Mrs. Smith greets each child as he or she enters the classroom.

Mrs. Smith, kneeling to look into Riley's eyes, "Riley, it looks to me like you're upset."

Riley mumbles softly: "Mommy said we have to move next week."

Mrs. Smith: "You're moving next week."

Riley: "Yeah. (very softly) But, I don't want to move."

Mrs. Smith: "You don't want to move."

Riley: "No, I like this school."

Mrs. Smith: "You like this school."

Riley: "Yeah."

Mrs. Smith: "You're sad about leaving."

Riley: "Yeah."

Mrs. Smith: "I can understand that moving would make you feel sad. You're going to miss your friends."

Riley: "Yeah." (pause) "Mrs. Smith, can I get a drink?"

Riley walks to the fountain to get a drink and moves to her seat to start work on the morning exercise. She is satisfied that her teacher understands why she is sad.

Mrs. Smith and Mrs. Varner were confronted with completely different situations. However, each teacher carefully reflected, using the child's exact words. Both Brooke and Riley felt validated because their teachers had listened to them.

It doesn't matter whether we are interacting with a young child, a teenager, or an adult; everyone wants to be understood. It also doesn't matter whether their situation is a sad or a pleasant one. Everyone needs someone to listen.

Something to think about . . .

Instead of answering questions that you are asked, take this opportunity to practice using each of the four responses to the questions that come your way in conversation this week (reflecting, deflecting, inspecting, and ignoring).

Chapter Nine

Getting to the Root of the Issue

Listen. Do not have an opinion while you listen because, frankly, your opinion doesn't hold much water outside of Your Universe. Just listen. Listen until their brain has been twisted like a dripping towel and what they have to say is all over the floor.

—Hugh Elliott

The Lord frees the prisoners. The Lord opens the eyes of the blind.

—Psalm 146:7b–8a

What goes on in the mind of a person who is trying to listen reflectively? Hopefully, the interaction between two friends, Phil and Jeff, will help us to better understand the conscious decisions a reflective listener makes during the listening process. Here are some of Phil's thoughts as he listens to Jeff.

Phil and Jeff have just run into each other on a Saturday morning at a local computer store. They begin with the usual light conversation about the weather and favorite sports teams. Finally, Jeff looks at Phil and says, "Phil, have you bought a computer lately?" Phil is an experienced listener and can quickly tell by Jeff's body language that this is not a light issue for him. Jeff's facial expression and tone of voice were quite serious as he asked the question. Phil is prepared to answer, but realizes it would be best to say, "I'm curious as to why you would ask that."

Jeff responds, "My wife and I have been looking for a new computer. You know a lot about computers and I was wondering if you could give me some advice."

Phil, sensitive to the tone of Jeff's voice and the strained expression on his face, says, "I'm interested in hearing what kind of computer you're looking for." Phil senses that the issue Jeff has presented is not the real issue. He realizes that if he gives Jeff advice at this point in the conversation, it will prevent Jeff from getting to the real issue. So, he inspects by giving Jeff the opportunity to offer more details.

Jeff: "I've done quite a bit of research. In fact, I've researched various brands of both desktop and laptop computers and I'm just not sure which one would be best. Once I think I have it narrowed down to one, I find another one that looks better. My wife, Jennifer, is upset with me. She wants me to just buy a computer since the one we have doesn't work most of the time. But I'm having a hard time making a quick decision."

Phil realizes that the conversation is becoming more personal. He invites Jeff to move to a nearby coffee shop where they will have more privacy. Once they are seated at a booth that provides freedom from distractions, Phil continues the conversation by reflecting on what he thinks is the most important issue for Jeff. "It sounds like you're having trouble deciding on the best deal."

Jeff: "That's it! I wish I could just buy one and be done with it. But I can't. Jennifer hasn't talked to me for two weeks because she is angry at me for not buying the cheapest computer I could find."

Phil, who has heard Jeff mention his wife's frustration for the second time, realizes that this is an issue he must address: "It sounds like your wife is really upset with you."

There is long period of silence. Phil is aware that this could be an important turning point in their conversation; therefore, he allows Jeff as much time as he needs to respond. Phil notices that Jeff's shoulders are slumped and that he looks down after speaking. He tries to imagine how Jeff must be feeling. The silence at this time is extremely vital. Jeff is deciding whether he wants to bail out of the conversation or move more deeply into the issue. Because Phil gives him time, he plunges to the deeper level.

Jeff comes out of the silence by looking at Phil and making a shocking statement: "Phil, Jennifer and I are getting a divorce. She hasn't talked to me for nearly a month. When I get any information from her, it comes from the kids. It really tears me up!"

It is Phil's awareness of his need to reflect and his ability to do so that enables Jeff to move from a seemingly simple challenge such as buying a computer to the more emotional and complex situation of his marriage possibly ending in divorce.

After a period of silence, Phil responds with "Wow. That must really be tough."

Jeff quickly answers, "It's the worst thing that's ever happened to me. I knew we were having some problems, but I never dreamed that Jennifer would go out with another guy!" He pauses and then says softly, "I never thought it would come to this."

Phil, dumbfounded, realizes he does not have an answer for Jeff and continues to reflect. "You're saying that Jennifer is dating another man."

Jeff, as he gazes past Phil: "Yeah."

At this time Phil decides to give Jeff some space (silence) and time to continue the conversation as he feels comfortable. What follows is a long period of silence during which both men are deep in thought. Jeff is thinking about his marital situation and Phil is thinking about how to continue to help his friend by using reflective listening. Finally Jeff says, "Do you know of any good marriage counselors?"

Again, Phil understands that answering Jeff's question is not the best response at this time. Instead, he allows Jeff to express what he's thinking and says, "It sounds as if you'd be interested in seeking counsel."

Jeff: "Well, we did go to see a friend of mine, but all he did was get on Jennifer's case. He told her to break it off with the other guy and to get back with me and the kids. She stormed out the door and took off in her car. Things got worse after that . . . that's when she moved out."

Phil: "You're saying that going to your friend for help made things worse."

Jeff: "Yeah. Up to that point she hadn't mentioned anything about getting a divorce. Now that's all she wants. I never thought it would come to this."

Phil: "Wow."

Jeff, glancing at his watch: "Phil, do you think we could get together again? I need help in dealing with this."

Phil: "You think that I might be able to help."

Jeff: "Yes, I do. You're the only person who has really listened to me so far!"

Phil: "Sure, I'd be glad to meet with you."

Phil senses that it would be best if he and Jeff would meet where they can have more privacy, so he decides to invite Jeff to his home.

Phil: "Why don't you come to my house for coffee around 9:00 next Saturday morning? Jamie and the kids will be shopping most of the day."

Jeff: "Sounds good! Boy, am I ever glad I ran into you today!"

Phil: "See ya' next Saturday at my place!"

This first conversation between these two friends reveals a problem in Jeff's life. Is it the real problem? Who knows? Jeff might go through many levels before he gets to the real issue or issues.

MOVING THE CONVERSATION TO A DEEPER LEVEL

The days following the interaction between Phil and Jeff are crucial for both men. Jeff finds himself pondering the things he has divulged to Phil. When Phil reflected the information and his feelings back to Jeff, it gave Jeff a clearer perspective of his situation. This phenomenon causes Jeff to think more deeply about the issues that are bothering him. Phil, on the other hand, is concentrating on how he can help Jeff by being a sincere listener. He contemplates how many times he wanted to ask questions or relate stories from his own life or even someone else's experience. And, of course, there was always the temptation to give Jeff advice. He thinks about how difficult it must be for Jeff to deal with a troubled marriage. In addition to this, Phil does one other very important thing: he prays for Jeff and Jennifer. He also asks God to give him wisdom as he listens to Jeff. During the week, he meditates on James 1:5 where we are encouraged to ask God for wisdom.

The following Saturday, Phil brews some coffee and arranges donuts and breakfast rolls neatly on a plate. He sits on his favorite chair in the living room to meditate and listen to the Holy Spirit. Jeff shows up around 9:10. Phil is aware of how uncomfortable this follow-up meeting could be for Jeff. Again, he puts himself in Jeff's position. He knows it's not easy for Jeff to express himself on such a personal level.

Jeff struggles with ambivalent feelings. He has a desire to talk, yet he is afraid of what might come out of his mouth as Phil listens. At first, both men talk about the weather and other less important things. After the two men are seated at the kitchen table, Phil pours two cups of coffee and addresses the issue they ended with the previous week by using an invitation to talk. He says, "I am wondering how things went for you this week." Jeff looks down with a sigh and mumbles, "It's been a pretty lousy week. Jennifer is pressing me to give her a divorce."

Phil focuses at this time on Jeff's body language. He notes that Jeff is hunched down in his seat and that he avoids eye contact. His head also hangs low as he speaks. He sounds discouraged and hopeless. Focusing on these nonverbal cues, Phil says, "I'm interested in how that makes you feel."

There is a long period of silence as Jeff struggles with his emotions. Several times Phil is tempted to tell him that his situation will work out all right but he knows that reassuring him at this point would be a stumbling block. Although he himself might feel better for saying it, it is doubtful that Jeff would actually find those words comforting. Besides, Phil doesn't know that things will work out. The situation could easily become worse before it gets better, if indeed it improves at all. Phil sits with Jeff during the silence and imagines how Jeff is feeling. After nearly forty-five seconds, he softly says, "Jeff, we don't have to talk about this if you don't want to."

Jeff looks up with tears in his eyes and says, "I really do need to talk about it. It's nearly killing me to watch my marriage go down the drain. Phil, it's all my fault! I haven't been a good husband. For years, Jennifer wanted me to go along for counseling but I refused because I didn't want to admit to anyone that we were struggling. You see, I cheated on her over five years ago. She forgave me and things got better for a while, but now she seems to resent what I did and is getting back at me."

Phil interrupts for clarification. "You're telling me that you believe this is all your fault."

Jeff: "Yeah. If I hadn't cheated on her we probably wouldn't be in this mess right now."

Both men sit in silence. Phil is wondering where this conversation will go and Jeff is deep in thought. Phil realizes that this period of silence is vital to their conversation. He struggles with the many questions he wants to ask but he knows that asking them would serve only to move the conversation in the direction that he wants it to go. This time he decides to allow Jeff to break the silence.

Finally, Jeff looks at him and asks, "What should I do?"

Phil says nothing. He hears the desperation in Jeff's voice and watches as he wrings his hands. He knows that he doesn't have any advice for Jeff, yet he's keenly aware that Jeff needs someone to help him wade through this issue. He senses an awesome responsibility as he realizes that he, Phil, is that person. Perhaps he is the only person Jeff can confide in.

Jeff continues, "I don't pray anymore. I'm pretty sure God doesn't love me. How could he love someone who cheated on his wife?"

WHEN THE COMMUNICATION TURNS

Whoa! Where did that come from? Phil is surprised at the sudden turn in conversation. He waits several seconds before reflecting because he senses that his next statement could possibly move the conversation to an even deeper level.

Finally he speaks. "It sounds as if you think God is angry with you."

Jeff responds, "I know He's angry with me. I'd have to be a fool to think otherwise!"

Phil decides to give Jeff more time to process his thoughts.

Jeff says, "I've certainly made a mess of my life." There is a long pause. "Phil, what should I do?"

Phil doesn't answer the question. Instead he responds, "I'm sure you've given some thought to that."

Jeff shocks Phil with his mumbled words: "Yeah . . . I could commit suicide."

Phil is speechless. He softly says, "You feel that that would solve the problem."

Jeff replies, "Yeah. Then Jennifer could marry the other guy and be happy."

Again, Phil does not respond, but continues to observe Jeff as he sits and stares blankly, making invisible circles with his restless fingers on the tabletop.

Jeff finally looks up and whispers, "I don't want to go to hell. I've been so depressed. Really, I've been depressed ever since Jennifer found out about my affair. She told me she couldn't stand living with someone who was always depressed. She nagged me all the time about going to church with her and the kids. I guess she just got tired of nagging and decided to move on with her life."

Phil waits silently for Jeff to continue.

"She told me that she forgave me, but I didn't believe it. I didn't understand how she could forgive a man who cheated on her."

Phil quietly challenges Jeff by saying, "It sounds to me like you haven't been able to forgive yourself."

Jeff looks up at Phil with surprise and blurts, "You know something, Phil? I think you're right. I think I've carried that guilt all these years. I've been angry with myself and, as a result, I've treated Jennifer and the kids very poorly. What should I do?"

This is at least the third time that Jeff has directly asked Phil what he should do. Fortunately, Phil has refrained from answering that question every single time. Phil now gives himself some time before responding. He realizes that the conversation is at a crossroads. It is tempting to tell Jeff what to do but he is not completely sure that they've reached the real issue yet. He finally says, "You're telling me that you want to know how to forgive yourself."

Jeff says, "That's it! How can someone forgive himself for being such a lousy husband and father?"

Again, Phil is tempted to tell Jeff what he thinks he should do, but he refrains. Instead, he reflects the statement that Jeff had made earlier: "You mentioned that Jennifer wanted you to go to church with her and the kids."

Jeff reacts quickly, "Yeah. I thought it was stupid being in church and being a sinner. I felt like such a hypocrite."

Phil reflects, "So, you feel like a hypocrite when you go to church."

Jeff reacts, "Wouldn't you?"

Phil doesn't answer. He decides to let Jeff make the next comment.

Finally, Jeff mumbles, "Phil, I've actually never become a Christian. I've always felt that Christians were a bunch of wimps. I could never go to the altar when the pastor asked people to go up for prayer. I didn't want anyone to see me there. I guess I was afraid that I'd break down or do something that would make me look stupid. I've always felt that only weak people needed Jesus."

Phil contemplates his next response and finally reflects, "It sounds like you think that Jesus is only for those who can't make it on their own."

There is a period of silence. Jeff needs time to think about Phil's reflection. He finally looks at Phil through tear-filled eyes and says, "Phil, I'm weak. I need Jesus. What do I need to do to become a Christian?"

Phil senses that they have now arrived at the real issue, and this time he feels free to answer Jeff's question. He asks Jeff to bow his head as they pray together for Jeff to receive Jesus Christ as his Lord and Savior.

This scenario is just one demonstration of a crucial listening experience. Phil focused on listening as Jeff weaved through many issues. Many times it would have been natural for Phil to give advice, to ask questions, or to talk about his own life or the life of someone else. But he never gave in to those temptations. He simply used reflective listening.

Does it mean that when we listen reflectively to another person all of his problems will be solved? Of course not. Jeff still has some serious issues to work through. However, the fact that Phil listened to him enabled Jeff to realize his need to receive Jesus into his life. Can Phil solve Jeff's problems? No, but Jesus can!

Phil listened and reflected as a friend struggled through a serious issue. Many of us think that we must do more than this, but the reality is that the most important thing we can do is listen. Asking questions, giving advice, self-editorializing, or reassuring may derail a person and prevent him from discovering the real issue. On the other hand, using reflective listening skills can provide the wings of liberty to a person who is struggling. Author John Eldredge reminds us that "the purpose of this thing called the Christian life is that our hearts might be restored and set free."[1] If we learn this skill, God will use us to impact lives for eternity!

Something to think about . . .

You can ask the Holy Spirit to help you make this prayer your own:

Father, let my existence be ruled by a great silence. Let my soul be listening, be given to the needs of others. Let me be silent in my innermost being, not asserting myself. Let my soul be detached, not grasping at anything in this world. And thus overcome in my life the power of habit, daily routine, dullness, fatigue and fear. Let me create within myself a careful tranquility, a place for every encounter, unreserved receptivity, and unhurried disposition. Extinguish within me the feelings of self-importance and the last stirrings of my ego, and make me gentle. Let me answer thoughts and situations rather than words. Through Jesus Christ our Lord, who taught us to be holy as you are holy. Amen.

—Hassan Dehqani-Tafti, exiled Iranian bishop

Chapter Ten

Listening with the Heart of God

Christians have forgotten the ministry of listening that has been committed to them by the One who is Himself the great listener.

—Dietrich Bonhoeffer in *The Cost of Discipleship*

But while knowledge makes us feel important, it is love that strengthens the church.

—1 Corinthians 8:1b

The ability to listen to others is extremely important. Unfortunately, we are often guilty of hurting others because we don't listen. This doesn't necessarily happen intentionally, but rather it is caused by the fact that most people do not know how to listen. Isn't it ironic that our society finds it necessary to spend millions of dollars to train and educate young people in many areas—years of education are required before receiving a high school diploma, weeks of practice are required and our skills are tested before we are allowed to drive a car, and so forth—but spends little money or time on educating people to communicate effectively by learning to listen? Why do we expect that the skill of listening should come naturally to us?

It seems that Christians especially feel that it is important to offer advice or quote Scripture to someone who seeks their help in dealing with a situation or an issue. There is an overwhelming desire to make the situation right or to attempt to make that person feel better. Here are some of the statements we make to people who are going through a difficult time.

- "God is in control."
- "Time heals all wounds."
- "All things work together for good to those who love God . . ." (a loose paraphrase of Romans 8:28).
- "This too shall pass . . ."
- "You need to have more faith . . ."
- "God is allowing this to happen for a reason . . ."

Although true, such comments do very little to encourage and reassure the person who is experiencing pain or sadness. Even Scripture verses can be used inappropriately or out of context.

Too often, we offer reassurances that cannot be guaranteed, such as the following:

- "By this time next week, it will all be over."
- "Tomorrow will be a brighter day."
- "Next year won't be as difficult . . ."
- "Things will get better soon . . ."
- "I'm sure it will be okay."
- "You'll make it through."

Not one of us has any control over these things. In reality, the situation could actually get worse for that individual. By making comments such as these, the listener is reassuring only herself, not the other person. In fact, the other person might leave the conversation feeling worse than she did before. She might even feel condemned—"I'm an idiot. Why do I feel this way?" Not only does she still face the same difficult or painful challenge, but she now has the added burden of having glib, matter-of-fact admonitions disguised as reassurances dumped onto her by someone who didn't know how to listen or validate the pain she was suffering.

Even praying for an individual who presents a need can, at times, be a stumbling block because it causes her to temporarily detour from getting to the real issue. We should pray for one another, but praying for the presenting problem is not effective. And, without listening, we may never find out what the real problem is! There are many times and places in which it is appropriate to give advice, quote

Scripture or pray with someone but, in order to fully demonstrate the love of Christ, sincere empathic listening should almost always come first.

A PERSONAL FAMILY STORY

Let me share the story of my daughter Robin, who was sexually abused by a family acquaintance. The situation did not come to light until several years later when Robin was in ninth grade. As our family dealt with this difficult issue, several individuals offered counsel. Well-meaning people told Robin that she needed to forgive the person who abused her. Others reminded her that God was in control and that everything would turn out all right. Thankfully, reflective listening enabled me to help Robin wade through the emotional pain she was experiencing. I listened often as she poured out her feelings. During one late-night conversation, Robin declared that some of her friends did not seem to care about her or her feelings. She believed they were concerned only with giving her "spiritual" clichés.

Fortunately, the Lord ministered to Robin through several people who consistently listened to her and did not judge what she said or give her simplistic responses. Eventually she was able to forgive her perpetrator and move on with her life. Today, Robin is happily married, the mother of four beautiful children, and is walking in victory.

There are far too many real-life examples of how well-meaning people who think they are being helpful or sensitive have instead, many times unknowingly, caused deep wounds by the words they said to a person who was already suffering from emotional pain. Another example of this is Sharon.

SHARON'S STORY

Sharon was in her late forties when she discovered that she had breast cancer. For five years, as she battled her illness, she also struggled with receiving advice from Christian friends. She was told frequently by people with good intentions that in order to receive physical healing she needed to have more faith. In fact, some individuals even insinuated that she had become sick because of sin in her life. As time passed, she avoided those people because she felt judged and condemned by them. Their constant advice and spiritual diagnoses demonstrated to her a lack of concern for her feelings and the issues she was attempting to work through. Fortunately, she did have a few Christian friends who didn't judge her or offer advice. One or two of those people listened daily as she expressed her fears and her struggles. Deep emotional healing took place in her life during the last year that she was alive. She eventually felt free to openly discuss her fears and disappointments with those who really listened. It was a very precious time for those who were skilled and willing to listen reflectively as she related both good and bad memories. Although she lost her five-year battle with cancer, this woman passed away peacefully because there were those who unselfishly offered their time and demonstrated compassion as they gave to her the precious gift of listening. I know her story well because Sharon was my first wife.

Unfortunately, experiences like that of my daughter and my first wife are all too common. Many people I have known throughout my life have shared similar experiences of not being listened to at a time in their lives when having a listener would have been very beneficial—a time when it was, in fact, necessary for their emotional health and well-being.

Many times I have listened to individuals weave through a number of presenting issues until they eventually get to the real issues that are bothering them. As they begin to honestly reveal the real problem, another issue emerges. Too often, that issue turns out to be the way that others have treated them in their time of crisis. Ironically, the pain and frustration that that person experiences as a result of insensitive comments is sometimes even more difficult for them to deal with than the emotional struggle surrounding their original problem. Sadly, it is usually a friend or relative who has unknowingly used one or more of the stumbling blocks at a time when the hurting individual needed someone to listen.

In most situations, people mean well and believe they are doing and saying the right things. (Right, meaning what is expected and appropriate.) They usually have the best intentions in the world. However, they can still be misguided and usually have no idea how hurtful some of their comments might be. But, ignorance is no excuse for hurting someone. A person generally makes a careless comment because she thinks that saying something is better than saying nothing at all in an uncomfortable situation.

THE STORY OF TIM

Several years ago, a man who had been experiencing some difficulties in his marriage came to see me. As Tim talked, I listened and reflected what I thought he was saying. Each time he came, we delved more deeply into his struggles and the pain he was experiencing. During his third visit, Tim told of an experience that he and his wife had had during a pastoral counseling session. The pastor had seemed more interested in fixing a computer problem in his office during their scheduled session than he had been in counseling them. He gave advice quickly and, without really listening, passed judgment on the communication patterns that Tim and his wife described. As a result of the pastor's divided attention and poor listening skills, Tim's wife was unwilling to return for counseling because she didn't believe that he really cared. In addition to preexisting marital conflict, this couple now experienced rejection and offense because someone who they assumed would help them, and who was in a position to do so, proved unable, or at the very least, unwilling. If the pastor did indeed care, the unfortunate truth is that he did not demonstrate this. What this couple in distress perceived very clearly was a lack of concern for them and their situation.

Unfortunately, the skill of reflective listening does not come naturally to most of us. Nor does it automatically come with a college degree or years of seminary training. It is not necessarily attached to most professions or vocations, though when it is absent from those in helping professions, it is most sorely missed.

What did I do to help Tim? I listened and reflected. And I listened again and reflected again, repeatedly. I approached the situation with the knowledge that I did not have the answers for him and his wife. I also knew that he needed someone to show him the love of Christ. His greatest resource would be someone with whom he could speak freely, who wouldn't judge him, who wouldn't give him advice or offer reassurances. He needed someone to listen with the heart of God. In this environment, he was able to honestly deal with his struggles.

After several months of listening to Tim, I found it interesting that he began to discuss his experiences with fellow Christians as they either criticized or advised him on what he needed to do to "fix" his marriage. He began to realize that receiving these reactions to his situation affected his relationship with those individuals in a negative way. He sensed that those people did not really care about him or his marriage.

In the world today, there are those who hurt others rather than help them. Many of them are not trying to hurt others but are trying to be helpful. If these individuals will learn to listen with love and compassion—and surely they can—they will begin to realize their potential for helping others and allow themselves to be used by God to heal broken hearts and bind up wounded lives.

The statement, "An individual won't care how much you know until he knows how much you care" is true. Listening to and walking with a person through a sensitive life issue is one of the greatest ways to demonstrate that we care. We are challenged by the apostle Paul to be like God—"Imitate God, therefore, in everything you do, because you are his dear children" (Ephesians 5:1). We are to strive daily to be compassionate and loving toward all those we meet. The great news is that we have God's strength to do this and the Holy Spirit to guide us as we listen.

I have often sensed that the Holy Spirit was giving me direction or insight as I listened to someone. Had I instead been focusing on a response or a solution or concentrating on offering reassurance, it is very likely that I would not have heard the Holy Spirit's still, small voice, nor might I have been willing to respond. In essence, one who sincerely listens will hear not only the speaker but the Holy Spirit as well.

Another important reminder about listening is that God's Word says that we are to "be happy with those who are happy, and weep with those who weep" (Romans 12:15). When we walk through a life issue with another person, we are, in some small way, fulfilling one of the commands of God's Word.

Listening allows one person to be truly human with another. It requires humility on the part of both the speaker and the listener. It also allows one person to love another by non-judgmentally walking alongside her. Listening reflectively affords an opportunity to demonstrate the love of Christ.

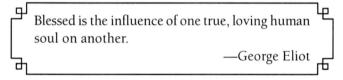

Blessed is the influence of one true, loving human soul on another.

—George Eliot

Several years ago, I received a phone call from a couple whose son had just been killed in an accident. Before I went to meet with this couple, my wife asked what I was going to do or say to comfort them. I told her that I was going to listen. And listen is exactly what I did as they, fraught with emotion, remembered past experiences and asked hard questions. Although some people might have seen this situation as a perfect opportunity to reassure them about the goodness of God, I did not use that approach. What amount of reassuring, questioning or advice-giving could even begin to ease the pain that they were surely experiencing at the loss of their only child? Instead, I chose to demonstrate the love of Christ by being a listening ear. I will always be convinced that listening reflectively can be a precious gift to a hurting soul.

Many of us find ourselves thinking, *I know I've hurt people because I didn't listen. What can I do?* I suggest that you go to the individual, if possible, and honestly admit that you now realize that you did not listen to her. Ask for her forgiveness and invite her to talk. Then, listen reflectively.

Even after years of practicing reflective listening, there are still times when I do not listen well. One particular incident stands out in my mind. A close friend and colleague had begun to tell me about a situation with his daughter, but I quickly took over the conversation. Later that evening, I realized that I had not listened to my friend. The next morning I went to him and asked him to forgive me for not listening. I then said, "Yesterday, you commented about your daughter's struggle. I'm wondering how that's going." He began to speak openly and, as I reflected this time, he was able to work through a difficult situation. I am so glad that I did not allow pride to prevent me from going back to my friend and offering him a second chance to talk. As a result, he and I have a wonderful relationship to this day.

> The central place for healing the soul is meant to be the local community of God's people, in ongoing relationships.
>
> —Dr. Larry Crabb

Many individuals approach my wife and me during our seminars with this same concern about not having listened reflectively. We suggest that after the seminar they go to the person to whom they did not listen and apologize, and then listen. Many of them contact us later to tell us how positive this experience was for them. When we do this, we build trust and respect in our relationship with that person.

A Word of Caution

We have no idea how much a person may be hurting, therefore, it is important to remember that listening to him or her can be easily misunderstood. If we listen to someone of the opposite sex we could become emotionally involved more easily than we realize. The act of listening can lead to an unhealthy intimacy if neither person protects his or her heart. Proverbs 4:23 admonishes, "Guard your heart above all else, for it determines the course of your life." The following situations I personally experienced may help us better understand what can happen as we listen reflectively to someone of the opposite sex.

Not Listening Responsibly

Shortly after I was introduced to the skill of reflective listening, I had the opportunity to listen frequently to a woman named Alice. I was eager to practice my reflective skills and she seemed pleased that I was willing to listen to her. Initially, Alice shared various concerns with me. As time progressed, she began to talk mostly about her marital problems. It felt good to know I was helping her work through some serious issues.

On one occasion, Alice began to relate how difficult the past weekend had been. During a long period of silence in which I was deliberating on how to respond to Alice's last statement, she looked at me and softly said, "I really enjoy talking with you." At first I thought nothing of her statement; however, I was shocked when she leaned forward and whispered, "My husband and I don't have a good sex life." At that moment, I realized that Alice and I had moved into dangerous territory and I quickly changed the subject.

That evening I explained to my wife what had happened between Alice and me. The next day I called Alice and told her that I would no longer be able to listen to her. That experience taught me to be very careful about listening to someone of the opposite sex. I saw first-hand how an innocent conversation can evolve into a dangerously intimate situation.

We must be wise listeners. There are times when it may be necessary to use a stumbling block to protect ourselves or the other person. I have personally made it a practice to be very cautious about listening to a woman if my wife is not present.

LISTENING RESPONSIBLY

The second experience illustrates how reflective listening can be a blessing in a healthy relationship. After my first wife's death, I didn't expect to marry again. One summer, Joanne, who is twenty years younger than I am, attended several professional development courses that I taught. After the third course ended, she invited me to visit her classroom to see how she was implementing some of the strategies she had learned in my courses. Since she was not married and I was a widower, I believed it was not inappropriate for us to have lunch together before going to her classroom. For three-and-one-half hours, I listened reflectively as Joanne revealed her dreams and desires. It was during this time that I realized what a beautiful person she was. I could feel myself becoming attracted to her. I felt certain that she did not have the same attraction for me and I was pretty sure that we would never see each other again. However (and fortunately for me), she accepted my invitation to meet for breakfast the following Saturday. As I listened to her again, I became even more attracted to her. When I disclosed my feelings, I discovered she was open to a relationship with me. To make a short story even shorter, we were married four months later! The fact that I chose to listen to her allowed us to become emotionally intimate, which has resulted in a wonderful marriage. However, if either one of us had been married at that time, those meetings would not have taken place.

If I had not taken the responsibility to stop the weekly meetings between Alice and me, it could have meant the destruction of many lives. Conversely, listening to Joanne gave me the opportunity to learn more about her. It also provided her with the understanding that I genuinely cared about her and wanted to know her better. We must be aware of the possible negative or positive results of listening to someone before we do so.

THE BLESSING OF REFLECTIVE LISTENING

I encourage us to be sensitive to the leading of the Lord as we become more effective as reflective listeners. Many times I have sat in amazement as the Holy Spirit has revealed the truth to a struggling individual. I like to think that the words of Jesus recorded in John 8:32 apply to the listening experience: "You will know the truth, and the truth will set you free." God wants to use us to help others find the truth and experience freedom.

The reality of being a Christian is that it is not about us—but it is about what God wants to do through us and how He will use us to bless others if we are yielded to Him. If we learn this skill and practice it daily, we will undoubtedly touch lives in dramatic ways. God will be able to use us in ways beyond our imagination! There are people in our lives right now who are silently begging *Please, Listen to Me!* Will you and I be the ones to respond? Will we be the ones to make a difference in their lives?

Something to think about . . .

We can ask the Holy Spirit to reveal to us
any individuals whom we have hurt in the
past by not listening to them. Then we can
ask God to forgive us and listen to Him to
find out if He wants us to approach any of
these individuals to ask for their forgiveness
also.

Where The Journey
Must Begin . . .

Perhaps you have picked up this book on a quest to begin the journey of reflective listening . . . but you realize that you don't have a personal relationship with the greatest Listener of all, Jesus Christ. There is hope . . . the God of the universe is waiting for you to seek Him . . . He's there when no one else is. He knows everything about you and He has wonderful plans for your life. He says to you, "In those days when you pray, I will listen" (Jeremiah 29:12).

In the book of Romans, the apostle Paul gives us several verses that explain our need for a Savior. These verses are sometimes called the "Romans Road to Salvation."

Romans 3:10 – "As the Scriptures say, 'No one is righteous—not even one.'"

Romans 3:23 – "For everyone has sinned; we all fall short of God's glorious standard."

Romans 5:12 – "When Adam sinned, sin entered the world. Adam's sin brought death, so death spread to everyone, for everyone sinned."

Romans 6:23 – "For the wages of sin is death, but the free gift of God is eternal life through Christ Jesus our Lord."

Romans 5:8 – "But God showed his great love for us by sending Christ to die for us while we were still sinners."

Romans 10:9-10 – "If you confess with your mouth that Jesus is Lord and believe in your heart that God raised him from the dead, you will be saved. For it is by believing in your heart that you are made right with God, and it is by confessing with your mouth that you are saved."

Romans 10:13 – "For 'everyone who calls on the name of the Lord will be saved.'"

Romans 8:1-2 – "So now there is no condemnation for those who belong to Christ Jesus. And because you belong to him, the power of the life-giving Spirit has freed you from the power of sin that leads to death."

Talk to God as you would to a close friend. Tell Him you are sorry for the wrongs you have done, and ask Him to forgive you. Receive His Son as your personal Savior and know that you have eternal life.

Open God's Word (the Bible) to learn more about Him and His great love for you. Read the Gospel of John to learn more about who Jesus is. Seek Him with all your heart and He will make Himself known to you.

Get involved with a group of believers who can encourage your spiritual growth. Find a Scripture-based, salvation-teaching church. Dig deeply into the Word of God. He will continue to reveal Himself to you!

Endnotes

Chapter One: What Is Reflective Listening?

1. Joseph Priestley
2. Reuel Howe, theologian and educator

Chapter Two: Our Belief System

Chapter Three: Stumbling Blocks to Effective Communication

1. Robert Bolton, *People Skills* (New York, NY: Simon & Schuster, Inc., 1979), p. 21-22.
2. Ibid, p. 22.
3. Ibid, p. 24-25.
4. Erin Linn, *I Know Just How You Feel . . . avoiding the clichés of grief* (Incline Village, NV, The Publisher's Mark, 1986), p. 97.

5. Robert Bolton, *People Skills* (New York, NY: Simon & Schuster, Inc., 1979), p. 90.

Chapter Four: Changing Questions to Statements

Chapter Five: The Invitation to Talk: Do's and Don'ts

1. Robert Bolton, *People Skills* (New York, NY: Simon & Schuster, Inc., 1979), p. 40.

Chapter Six: The Reflective Listening Process

1. Robert Bolton, *People Skills* (New York, NY: Simon & Schuster, Inc., 1979), p. 33.
2. Ibid, p. 39.

Chapter Seven: Silence Is Golden

Chapter Eight: Handling Questions Presented by the Speaker

1. Robert Bolton, *People Skills* (New York, NY: Simon & Schuster, Inc., 1979), p.51.

Chapter Nine: Getting to the Root of the Issue

1. John Eldredge, *Waking the Dead: The Glory of a Heart Fully Alive* (Nashville, TN, 2003), p. 113.

Chapter Ten: Listening with the Heart of God

About the Author

Richard "Dick" E. Fetzer, Sr., M.Ed. is the fourth of five sons born to Dean and Cora Roan Fetzer. He grew up on a small farm in Centre County, Pennsylvania. His mother, a quiet person who listened with patience and understanding, was a great influence in his life. The seeds to becoming an effective listener were sown in Dick's life as he spent time helping her around the house since she was ill for much of her life.

Dick earned a bachelor's degree in elementary education from Shippensburg University and a master's degree in education from West Chester University. He taught various elementary grade levels in the public school system for thirty-five years, and also coached wrestling.

While in his late twenties, two significant events had an impact on Dick's life. The first and most important event was accepting Jesus Christ as his personal Lord and Savior. The second event occurred several months later when he attended a series of workshops at Lock Haven University. It was at one of these workshops where he was introduced to reflective listening. He sensed that God was guiding him to learn this skill, and he did so by praying, practicing diligently, and pursuing further training.

After his retirement from the public school system, Dick joined the faculty at Lock Haven University of Pennsylvania as a professor in the Early Childhood Education department. He later transferred to the Elementary Education department.

Dick and his first wife, Sharon Tressler, raised three children—Rebecca, Richard, Jr., and Robin. After nearly thirty-two years of marriage, Sharon went to be with the Lord. Shortly afterward, Dick met and married his present wife, Joanne Freed. They are blessed to have ten grandchildren.

In 2003, Dick and Joanne founded *People to People Ministries*, a ministry through which they offer seminars on learning styles and communication skills.

Dick enjoys a variety of outdoor activities—gardening, golfing, swimming, and listening to God while riding his bicycle.

For more information on *People to People Ministries*, please contact:

People to People Ministries
108 North Hampton Street
Lock Haven, PA 17745-2422
Phone: (570) 748-4899
email: p2pmin@verizon.net
website: www.peopletopeopleministries.org

Printed in the United States
202736BV00001B/22-81/P